ESCAPE IS AT HAND

TALES OF A BOY AND A BAND

JOSHUA KLOKE

ETERNAL CAVALIER PRESS

EC

Published in Canada by Eternal Cavalier Press.

LIBRARY AND ARCHIVES CANADA CATALOGUING IN PUBLICATION DATA

Kloke, Joshua, 1983-, author
Escape is at hand: tales of a boy and a band / Joshua Kloke.

ISBN 978-0-9919660-0-4

I. Title.
PS8621.L64E82 2013 C813'.6
C2013-902790-4

www.eternalcavalierpress.com

Cover design by Dustin Pringle
Cover photo by Joshua Kloke

2nd Edition

Printed in Canada.

For my parents

"Loosen your collar,
shake off the wires.
Run like a river,
glow like a beacon fire."

-"Young Lions," Constantines

Foreword

Let's be honest: we Canadians have historically been miserable gits when it comes to rallying behind Canadian artists. For decades—the '60s and '70s were especially bad—we had this misguided egalitarian attitude towards anyone who would dare be a star. "Who do you think you are?" was the prevailing attitude—unless, of course, an artist found success in America. That bit of external validation made us quick to say "Yes! That's one of ours."

Fortunately, though, we've become much, *much* better at embracing our own. While we're exporting more internationally acclaimed artists than ever before, it's also possible for an act to have a successful and sustainable domestic career.

The Tragically Hip are perhaps the best example of this change in attitude. Although they have plenty of fans in other territories and sell decent amounts of music and concert tickets elsewhere, it's at home where they are genuine capital 'S' Superstars. Sold out tours. Constant radio airplay. Massive anticipation for each new release.

And it's hard to find a more quintessentially Canadian band. With lyrical references to Canadian people, landmarks, events (and, of course, hockey), their love for Canada is worn on their sleeves—and the country loves them back.

The Hip have been big enough and around long enough to have had a serious impact on several generations of music fans. Some of these people are so deep into the band's culture that like Deadheads, Parrot Heads and the fellow travellers who follow U2 around the planet, a big part of their identity is Hip Fan.

This is one of those stories. If you've followed The Tragically Hip at any point since 1987, you may find what you're about to read rather familiar.

— Alan Cross
April 2013

Introduction

The conversation always starts the same way. I meet someone, we exchange pleasantries and eventually discuss our jobs. I tell him or her that I'm a music writer. We start talking music. In order to find a common ground, we cover the larger bases: genres we enjoy and artists we identify with.

Once I was asked, within minutes of meeting someone, to name my All-Time Top Five Desert Island records (though I later found out this person just wanted to get closer to the friend I had brought to the party). Most music fans have enough sense to understand the magnitude of this question. But within a minute or two of this discussion, the question is inevitably asked: "So who's your favourite band, then?"

And then I'm caught on a social tightrope, wondering two things:

One: How much information should I divulge?

Two: How much does this person even want to be talking to me?

The question makes me nervous because I can't give a simple answer without any kind of story to go along with it. Friends within earshot of the question roll their eyes and offer the person a way out.

Depending on my mood, I might mutter something about The Detroit Cobras or The Rolling Stones. Looking back on my obsession, I can now admit that there are other bands out there. Though really, how could anyone explain half a life's worth of devotion to a band to someone they've just met without sounding like they belong to a cult?

If I was to tell the truth, I could not leave it at three words. I could not help but tell this person that The Tragically Hip, a seminal five-piece rock and roll band out of Kingston, was the band that served as the soundtrack to my youth. The band that I followed across two continents. The band whose music I lost my virginity to. The band that got me into music writing.

But I can't squeeze these pivotal moments into a conversation that would probably last the length of a pop song. Even if I tried, it's unlikely anyone would understand. There are certain things in life that, while seemingly trivial to others, carry too much emotional weight to be summed up in three minutes.

I was a kid when I was introduced to The Tragically Hip but my relationship with the band has grown and evolved, and taught me more than any schooling ever could. I had a typical upbringing in the suburbs of Southern Ontario. Were it not for The Hip (as they shall be referred to from here on in), it's doubtful I would have ever left my hometown. I was not looking for love when I stumbled onto The Hip but their music has evolved into a language that has taken me close to twenty years of emotional involvement to comprehend. Like so many music fans who grow attached to a band, I heard that language when others did not. I followed that language through concerts, cities, countries, and continents. I followed it through soft drugs and more than my fair share of booze. I lost girlfriends and good friends and generally remained unaffected by the belief that there was a way of life that didn't involve being a dedicated fan. I learned a lot along the way; all great art inherently teaches.

And though my obsession was born of my own accord,

there were still rules to be followed. The language that The Hip spoke kept me constantly trying to discover what those rules were. The rules aided me in my search to better understand the band, the world around me and myself. So to you, I present those rules.

In the early '90s it was easy to believe that a rock and roll band could save the world. So I pity kids who don't allow themselves to dream. Cynicism is always right around the corner, but rock and roll provided me some flexibility.

For (supposedly) the best years of my life I was obsessed with the music and mythology of The Hip. I wouldn't be who I am without them. But I was lucky, not only was I obsessed with the band, I was obsessed with what they taught me.

CHAPTER 1

Dive in Headfirst

"Thank you. We are never going away."

It's been a long time since I first heard Gord Downie, lead singer of The Hip, deliver that line to me back in the cheap seats of a massive hockey arena. Though I now understand the line in context, being only sixteen its historical aspects flew over my head. I knew then that I'd missed out on a lot at my age. Having an affinity for history, it feels like I'm playing catch-up most of the time. So let's start at the beginning.

My earliest memory of The Hip dates back to 1993. It was a typical summer of my youth. My father and I were driving to a soccer game sometime after dinner. My father was the enduring and tolerant coach of my park league team and these drives were vital to our relationship; on the field, we barely spoke.

As I was only ten years old and my musical tastes were in their embryonic stages, my father controlled the conversation and the radio stations. CFNY in Toronto, then known for its progressive programming, was the station of choice. And it was hard to escape The Hip in 1993. Having just released their third full-length album, chock-full of their unique brand of meat and potatoes rock, the band's star-status was rising in the Great White North.

From the shitty speakers in our 1992 Chevrolet Corsica, a chunky groove blared. It was the groove that first caught my attention; when I was on the soccer field I always believed I had a mental edge if I kept a driving, motivating song in my head for the entire game. It was fuel. And that day, the song would be "Fifty Mission Cap." It's a song that ignites a fist-pumping fervour, though I've also seen many a crowd emit clouds of pot smoke during the opening chords.

Without any expertise in rolling a joint just yet, I was left only to listen. I nodded along; lucky for me I already had embarrassing straps around my glasses that prevented them from falling off during a game. My mother wouldn't let me leave the house without them, but was thoughtful enough to buy them in colours that matched my uniform.

As I got caught up in the tune, I stopped listening to my father's advice. At times I hated soccer; all my friends (and it seemed every boy across Canada) were playing hockey. In 1993, soccer resided on the fringe of boyhood pastimes. And here was a culture shifting song about hockey that made me doubt my own pastime even more:

> "Bill Barilko disappeared/That summer/He was on a fishing trip/The last goal he ever scored won the Leafs the cup/They didn't win another until 1962/The year he was discovered…"

Later in my boyhood, this tune took on even more relevance, as I became enamoured with all things Toronto sports. The Blue Jays were at the height of their fame, and thanks to the acquisition of Doug Gilmour (a Kingston native no less—in the eyes of a ten-year-old boy the world seemed entirely within reach) the Maple Leafs were a good enough team to throw my high-pitched voice behind.

I might have just enjoyed the groove had my father not seen my heightened enthusiasm and spoken up.

"D'you know these guys?" he asked me. His hands remained at ten and two, his eyes still focused on the road.

"Nope."

My hands drummed on the dashboard. I stared down

into my short shorts. (Praise the designer who realized those shouldn't remain popular.)

"They're called The Tragically Hip. They're from Canada. Kingston, I think. This song's about a guy that used to play for the Leafs."

Although I wasn't a short kid, my father was a giant. I'd heard him wax poetic on various subjects before (a prerequisite of fatherhood, I'm sure) but today was the first time he had dabbled in musical knowledge. I'd browsed his record collection a few times; the standard mix of prog-rock staples that seemed commonplace in the record collections of men his age.

It was rock and roll. But it was unlike anything I'd ever heard.

There was a mystery within "Fifty Mission Cap." And in 1993, before the internet, mystery wasn't readily available for a young boy in the suburbs. Downie's lyrics contained a cryptic message that seduced me.

Soon after that day, a cassette copy of *Fully Completely*, The Hip's landmark third record, found its way into our home. "Fifty Mission Cap," the ninth track on the record, became a household staple. I tried day after day to recapture the original anthemic, sweeping feeling I'd had in the Corsica.

I've since nailed the source of the cassette, too. Word had travelled after that fateful car ride from my father, the coach, to my uncle, the assistant coach. (My grandfather's family motto: stick the fuck together.) Earlier that summer, my uncle had taken a trip to Australia by his lonesome. In an attempt to keep his nationalistic blood running warm, *Fully Completely* served as the soundtrack for his trip. Everyone's got that "cool uncle" and mine introduced me to a collection of songs that would change my life for the better.

It would be six-and-a-half years before I'd experience the outright bliss of hearing "Fifty Mission Cap" live. For the time being, that song and the hockey card that inspired it were my sole connection to the band. At ten years of age, all I knew of heroes (especially Canadian ones) was that they were to be worshipped, case closed. And Bill Barilko, whose number five jersey hung in retirement, was a hero of the highest order.

"Fifty Mission Cap" at first listen is nothing more than a rallying call for Toronto Maple Leafs fans, yet the tragedy Gord alludes to in the song's lyrics (Barilko disappearing suddenly on a fishing trip in Northern Ontario) demanded a deeper examination of Barilko's mythology.

In a 2004 radio interview, Hip guitarist Rob Baker commented on the difference between the way Americans and Canadians treat their cultural icons.

"Americans tend to build up their heroes," he said. "Whereas Canadians tend to tear them apart."

"Fifty Mission Cap" began for me as a purely straightforward tale, though eventually I saw how The Hip were telling it in a not so straightforward manner.

Still, in that moment the percussion was prominent and heavy; it was easy to bang along on anything within reach. This was the formula: grunting and smashing in rhythm, not unlike how chimps might have created music in the first place. It makes sense; this was the beginning of an evolution.

◆◆◆

The timing was right for this song to enter my life. At the tender age of ten, when girls still remain foreign, boys need hobbies. For me, it was collectable sports cards.

I stuck to hockey and baseball cards and Upper Deck was my brand. But Pro-Set was Gord's brand, apparently. That's where you can find the card from which he stole the story for "Fifty Mission Cap" (Pro-Set 91/92, #340). So it gave hope to my little hobby. I spent entirely too much of my parents' money on sports cards, yet now I had a plausible argument to throw in their faces every time they scoffed at donating another five bucks to my cause. If this new hero, this icon of all things good and Canadian, could find meaning in a hockey card, then surely there was some purpose in building a collection of my own?

I gradually moved away from hockey cards and into

rock music, playing the hell out of that *Fully Completely* cassette. For a time, it was the only actual cassette I owned besides a slew of taped-from-radio compilations.

Slowly, the conversations between my father and me on the way to the field deteriorated. I'd still listen to his directions, but often with only one ear. Maybe it was inevitable, but that summer paved the way for a different kind of enthusiasm. I'd never cared so much about music beyond simplistic rhythms before "Fifty Mission Cap." I'd never heard a song that compelled me enough to actually investigate it.

The first time I heard the song live was in the Air Canada Centre, which at the time was the new home of the Toronto Maple Leafs. It was my first Hip gig. When the song closed the first encore, the lights flooded over the crowd and I saw thousands of hands banging against the person next to them and heard thousands of voices singing wildly. It had been almost seven years from when I first heard "Fifty Mission Cap" on the radio to that moment. And it took nearly every day of those seven years for me to realize exactly what I was a part of. At most rock and roll shows, standing is a prerequisite. But only at the end of a truly rousing number, when the entire crowd raises their hands, does the band get anything close to a "standing ovation." It's the fans trying desperately to stretch taller than they are out of sheer appreciation.

I smiled, sang along with my awkward teenage friends, and banged against the rails in the hopes of getting in on this uniting act of love. This was how everyone around me was reacting, and being a virgin to this kind of experience, I was at a loss for composure. So I did what felt right and once again locked into the song's groove. I hung over the rail and felt the chorus work its way through my butterfly-infested stomach and out through a crackly voice.

The song hit its historical climax:

> "The last goal he ever scored/Won the Leafs the Cup…"

A spotlight shone towards Barilko's retired jersey. If we

as a crowd couldn't sing in tune, we sure could hoot and holler generously.

> "They didn't win another until 1962/The year he was discovered/It's my Fifty Mission Cap…"

Before Downie walked offstage he left the crowd with that simple, enduring mantra:

"Thank you. We are never going away."

The first thing I did when returning home after the concert (after my standard late-night meal of cereal and potato chips) was jot down what I remembered of the setlist. Before bed, I rooted through my old cards and found the inspiration for the song. Eventually, I would begin the time-honoured tradition of interpreting (and truly believing) The Hip's lyrics to suit events in my own life and using the lyrics to mirror my own development and maturity. But for the time being, I was elated with the first contact I'd made.

At the Air Canada Centre, I was only one of thousands of voices, indistinguishable from any other. But this was the band's way of communicating to their fans: bringing stories and methods from the past to the forefront and allowing those who trusted the band to form their own connection.

Here was a new hobby that nineteen thousand fans, a piece of Canadian history, a few musicians on a stage and two brothers had helped me discover. But it was up to me to understand what everyone was screaming about. And as Gord Downie had alluded, I'd have lots of time to do just that.

"[The Tragically Hip] are in a position to help other bands. It's pretty easy for you not to help other bands if you're in the position that they are. To not think to reach out. But they've always been very thoughtful guys. For [Tragically Hip bassist Gord Sinclair] to come out to our shows in Kingston and offer up their space to record and give us an awesome deal to record there; obviously they're running a business but they don't need to be as generous as they are."

— Max Kerman, Arkells

CHAPTER 2

Learn From Your Elders

I became a massive fan of The Hip through an unconventional route. Sure, the radio was involved, but to have my father and my uncle aid my discovery of the band was, at the time, supremely uncool. Punk fans would have me crucified.

Yet learning about the band from my elders, in retrospect, makes sense. After all, The Hip have plied their craft with respect for their elders. Even when the band was relatively young, they were peerless yet still heavily influenced by bands that came before them. They attained a level of class that fans and critics usually only grant to the elder statesmen of rock and roll. And though the majority of the band had yet to reach their thirtieth birthdays, when I discovered their music, they already were those elders.

In 1993, having only released three full-length albums, The Hip embarked on an ambitious cross-Canada tour: the inaugural "Another Roadside Attraction," where they played festival-style gigs to hordes of fans in large, dusty outdoor venues. By choosing veteran Aussie rockers Midnight Oil as their opening act, The Hip showcased an appreciation for their influences to the largest audience they'd ever had.

Lead guitarist Rob Baker's solos owe so much to the plight of old bluesmen that it's easy to imagine him playing alone on a stool well into old age. (Friends of mine affectionately call him, "the one who looks like Jesus." Can you really get more elderly than that?) And while The Hip would never turn down a young fan, the band's longevity, combined with their resistance to flash-in-the-pan musical trends, won't be winning over too many of the Twitter generation anytime soon.

Talk of The Hip being an "old band" gets me teary-eyed and longing for the mid '90s, when I had to fight for them in arguments about music up against the heavyweights of the day like Green Day and Nirvana. (Though really, which of these three bands has aged most gracefully?) My obsession started at a young age and was aided by the fact that I had my back against the wall. I was ridiculed by friends for admitting that I liked a band that their fathers liked, but that's probably why I enjoyed being in the company of my elders at Hip gigs: I had a lot to learn from them.

◆◆◆

Hip fans can be a precarious bunch. Mix emotionally charged followers with more than a few drinks and often, you've got a recipe for disaster. What's more, The Hip are a favourite with the hockey and rugby crowds, which should give you an indication of the intimidation a naïve, bespectacled youngster was dealing with at his first few gigs.

But every so often you meet one of the good guys: a fan whose dedication to the band and outward charm enhances everyone else's experience. These concert characters don't just add to the atmosphere, they help to create it. The intense, short-term relationships you can form with these other fans only reaffirm your faith in the pseudo-religious power of the band itself.

I had first heard of Hugh, the well-built firefighter with a hearty chuckle, through Hip internet message boards (which I've spent more time on than I'd like to admit). His concise but emotional reviews of shows had fans salivating at every detail. Boisterous and full of luck, he found his way backstage after every gig he attended. I had to meet this guy. I wanted to learn from those who felt the same passion and responsibility to maintain the aura of a great gig that I did, but with more fruitful results.

The chance presented itself in the summer of 2003 at Molson Park in Barrie. I was to be introduced to Hugh through a friend from the message boards. With one of the many opening bands onstage, I approached Hugh and his party. He had an immense presence and a sharp, grey haircut that could cut through the toughest steak. To this day I don't know what band was playing, but Hugh stayed fixated on the stage, swaying in a languid and hypnotic way, though not in sync with the band.

I was introduced by our mutual friend. "Hey Hugh, this is Joshua. He's been wanting to meet you."

Hugh barely blinked. It didn't matter who was onstage. This was Hugh's gig. I stood mystified.

"Oh, don't worry," offered the friend. "He always gets like this at Hip shows."

I left, still bewildered. When the sun finally set and The Hip were about to hit the stage, I felt a rush of pre-show butterflies. Ashley, a good friend of mine who was taking in her first Hip gig, smiled and confessed, "You know, I've been looking forward to seeing The Hip. But even more, I've been looking forward to seeing what happens to you when they come onstage."

Under the moonlight, The Hip took the stage and I fell into a trance. My limbs moved of their own volition. I had taken notes and now I was suspended under the air of a surprise "Fire in the Hole." There was no controlling me. Having met other dedicated fans and learned from their ways, I immediately felt accepted. I floated without conceit or embarrassment.

On the two-and-a-half hour ride home, right before she passed out, Ashley confessed a little more: "It was everything I hoped it would be."

"The gig or my reaction?"

She snored a little and muttered, "Both."

I chuckled to myself, thanking this Hugh guy I'd never met.

◆◆◆

Almost a year to the day, I finally met Hugh properly at the Odeon in Cleveland. After a messy gig the night before, I knew I had to channel his passionate and focused frame of mind. But upon meeting him in line, he acted as if he didn't know me. I said to myself, "Oh, don't worry. He always gets like this at Hip shows."

Inside the musty 850 person capacity club, I stood with Hugh against the front rail. I wanted advice on how to balance exuberance with focus. Standing beside a true, upstanding Hip fan was a lesson in dedication.

"Hey Hugh," I said. "I'm going for a beer. You want one?"

"No thanks. I'm holding the spot."

I was humbled. Instead of returning with two beers as I normally would have, I slowly sipped one while watching openers the Sam Roberts Band. Perhaps taking in a show sober was the key to ingesting as much atmosphere as possible. I had so much to learn. And that night at the Odeon would provide no shortage of opportunity to become well versed in just how aware a true fan must remain at a concert.

The Hip were well into their set when catastrophe struck.

◆◆◆

Violence in the crowd will forever be a blemish on the face of rock and roll. Being the Stones fans that they are, the band has likely seen *Gimme Shelter*. And surely, The Hip felt the shock of the Roskilde tragedy in 2000 that almost ended Pearl Jam's career.

At the 1998 Grape Jam Festival in Erie, the band was charging through the intro to what was destined to be a legendary "Fire in the Hole." Though I wasn't in attendance, the night is well documented thanks to a pristine-sounding bootleg that's a mainstay in any Hip fan's collection. The band rollicked towards the musical equivalent of Armageddon. The fence at the front had proved to be rather light and Gord Downie had warned the crowd a number of times about its failing durability. And as the band pummelled through "Fire in the Hole," it turned into one of their landmark moments, for all the wrong reasons.

As fans rushed the stage, Downie continued to warn them in his cryptic manner that what they were crushing was "just a snowfence." The song continued to surge. It was time for the enigmatic lead singer to drop the famous opening line, normally delivered with frantic force:

> "You triumphed over will/You had immunity to kill"

Instead, he called the band to a halt. He drew boos from the crowd and the band walked offstage. Not the most electrifying of moments from the festival's headlining act.

Back then, The Hip weren't just teetering on the verge of mass-market (or better yet, American) stardom (the band's only record review ever published in Rolling Stone magazine being 1998's *Phantom Power*) but their approach to live sets was also in a state of flux. Would they pump out chugging numbers like "Courage" for the moshers and crowd-surfers? Or would the band risk alienating those fans with gems like "Thompson Girl," an acoustic number that ensured the safety of those smaller, braver fans who made the trek up to the front? It was a delicate balance for the band and especially Gord Downie, whom nearly every crowd treats with godlike reverence.

The Hip have always maintained loyalty to their fans. Regardless of how far you've come for the band, how many times you've seen them or how many bootlegged B-sides you've listened to, their expansive live sets create a sense of equality within the crowd. From the cheap seats to the front row, every fan is there for the same reason and is treated with the same respect. It's a safety and comfort that many artists strive for, but is rarely attained. Although it lacks a punk ideal, when I stand at a Hip gig looking around like a child might, I feel a strange but reassuring protection from the five band members onstage. The Grape Jam gig was one of the few at which the band have had to leave the stage prematurely. But forgoing contractual obligations and potentially sacrificing payment in exchange for the safety of their fans seems more important in the long run.

◆◆◆

Back in Cleveland, The Hip led the sweaty masses through another sonically charged "Fire in the Hole" to finish their second encore. I had been wondering if there was something I could do to cement my place up front for all eternity. I noticed a smallish, dirty blonde girl who'd only been up front since the first encore. For her, preserving the moment in her memory meant clambering over the four-foot barrier (overzealous, but her intentions seemed pure), then falling and smashing her head on the cement.

Everyone up front peered over the barrier as she lay there, motionless. A few security chumps slowly wandered over to inspect her. Being a small club, all of this happened in plain view of the band. And still, in the distance now, was a stretching "Fire in the Hole." Were we together, as a crowd, to bear witness to a wondrous night that could soon turn ugly?

Fully aware of the young woman who had injured herself in an effort to become even more absorbed into his band's unwavering intensity, Downie moved stage right, choosing to sing to the opposite side of the venue. He was unable to watch. Gord Sinclair kept time on his bass all too precisely, watching over the stage. The rest of the band charged along, yet an eerie tension had taken over. This night was about to take a dreadful turn. We needed a hero.

Showing little regard for his own safety, Hugh jumped over the barrier. The security guards awoke from their sleepwalking, but Hugh wasn't about to let the louts stand in his way. "I'm a paramedic!" he screamed, fighting them off. He held the girl cautiously and the seconds on the clock began to tick again. Though what was happening was only visible to those up front, a sense of calm returned to the band. As Hugh pulled the girl up from the ground, Gord returned to his position and let his pent-up emotion loose on the crowd to finish a deafening "Fire in the Hole." Hugh disappeared into the crowd with the girl in his arms and didn't return for the rest of the gig. It had become a memorable night but only because the band and Hugh had worked together to make it so.

Every night, small venues like the Odeon pack sweaty, eager fans into a perfect square, getting them high on the smell of sweat and smoke machines. Older fans that have to get up early the next day and those dragged to the club by other devotees hang out together on the balcony, sipping drinks. The dressing rooms might be too small for the bands, but that doesn't matter to the fans up front. This night, whether it's a Sunday before exams or the Friday after you just got fired, will be the greatest night of your life. It's in these clubs that fans like me feel at home.

Some bands want fans to stroke their egos endlessly. But I understood how Hugh had become a revered figure in Hip subculture and always made it backstage. I'd envied those fans and wondered if I'd ever become one. The Hip respected Hugh because he did everything in his power to take care of his fellow fans. You couldn't ask a twenty-one-year-old stoner like me to do that. Only someone who loves the music enough to ensure its continuity can be depended on. The real fans: the elder statesmen.

After the gig ended, I inched past the merchandise stand and saw a small group gathering around the bar. There, standing with the thirsty horde was opener Sam Roberts, whose shaggy disposition was becoming a fixture of everyman rock. Over a Heineken, Sam and I shot the shit about his last date in my university town of Guelph. He even claimed to remember my polite but supportive vocal outburst. And although Hugh had been the star of the night, I was beginning to carve out a Cleveland story of my own.

As our conversation wound down, Sam asked how a kid from Guelph had managed to make his way to gigs in Detroit and Cleveland without any visible friends or a vehicle. Now, had the Gods of Rock and Roll presented Sam to me earlier in the day, I would have been sheepish, mumbling that I'd hitched a ride with a few folks I'd met on the internet. But that morning was so long ago. Instead, I boasted, "I just had to get to these gigs. I hooked up with some dudes on The Hip's message board and they offered me a ride. Last night we stayed at a bullet-riddled room in Detroit. Real rock and roll. Another member of The Hip's message-board clan, Hugh something, set it up. And it's all been worth it, without a doubt." I smiled, feeling proud of myself.

Sam replied, "Oh, no way! Hugh is here? I gotta find that guy!"

"[The Tragically Hip] are an institution in Canadian rock 'n' roll music. They're an anomaly in terms of mainstream success and mainstream radio-friendly bands. We were all just excited because they seemed interested in us. It was a connection to something with an interesting history. We all saw them as a real band. A band that started in bars and developed an audience based on being an interesting band more than anything else, which is surprisingly rare."

— Bry Webb, Constantines

CHAPTER 3

Take Chances

Fans of The Tragically Hip may be testosterone-driven goons who drink to excess and provide the hooting and hollering necessary to elevate a crowd, but they can also be quiet, patient geeks who prefer the band's solemn language to be spread not across a packed hockey arena but across coffee houses with a few acoustic guitars and other equally patient music geeks.

Those stereotypes occupy the outer edges of The Hip's circle of fans but there's a mess of others united in their passion for the band—and often nothing else. The Hip have been touring for close to twenty-five years, and their fans run the gamut of the human condition. Bands that have built a legacy on making personal connections (Pearl Jam is another example) won't just attract one specific type of person.

While art may not initiate the spirit of competition, being a dedicated fan does funny things to a person. It was a friend of my sister's who first asked me, "Why do Hip fans always try to out-Hip each other?"

Though I didn't want to admit it at first, her question was valid.

The band's legacy is inescapable in that they've touched

so many lives and Hip fans always clamour for a better story: Who's seen the better gig? Who's been to more gigs? Who's met the band before and under what circumstances? And whose mother's drycleaner had once stood behind Paul's babysitter at a Starbucks in Kingston? Every Hip fan has a story. By 2004, mine were still fairly run of the mill.

I'd been a Hip fan for ten years and been going to gigs for four but my stories didn't amount to shit. I knew I was the world's biggest Hip fan (I had the posters, put up against my housemates' wishes, to prove it) but I'd only seen the band at massive Ontario shows. My story was the same as thousands of other kids. I'd met fans who had followed the band across the United States, catching them in venues the size of an arena's bathroom. They'd rave about how intimate the experience was and how it was the only "real" way to see the band.

Though I knew every lyric to every track and could mimic every guitar lick and every one of Gord's mumbling rants on every bootleg I owned, I was still light-years away from really knowing the band. Standing hundreds of feet away from the stage at Molson Park in Barrie the previous summer, the band appearing only slightly bigger than my thumbnail, I felt like a fraud. There must be something more, I thought; an untapped source of emotional gratification that, given my proximity to the United States in 2004, was finally attainable.

If I was to prove to myself that I truly did love this band, I'd have to make some sacrifices. I wouldn't be driving my father's new Grand Am across the border, bringing close friends along for the ride. I could have gone it alone but I'd have risked a personal monetary knockout that just wasn't feasible for a third-year university student. I was dedicated, but torn.

I took to The Hip's online community. A little research presented me with an opportunity: in late September, I could hitch a ride down to Detroit from my home in Guelph with three Hip fans out of Toronto (none of whom I'd ever met) for a gig at the legendary Fox Theatre. We would press on to Cleveland the next day, for the aforementioned Odeon gig.

I made the arrangements and bought the tickets in a span of about ten minutes; no second thoughts. I didn't let my friends or housemates know where I was headed for fear of being (rationally) convinced otherwise. This was not a trip I could share; this was something I had to indulge in for myself, without any recourse.

When that fateful September morning arrived, I slipped out of my house undetected and into a Honda Civic. Chris, the balding, eager leader of our troupe, seemed like the kind of person who had been a world-class Boy Scout. He kept the momentum going and ensured that everything went according to schedule. He had also brought an impressive video recording rig to document the gigs for the enjoyment of other Hip fans. He was not the hoot-and-holler type. His passion was systematic.

Trevor, Chris's best friend, was the ebullient type. Always cracking wise, his smile stretched across borders. I knew right away that I'd get along just fine with Trevor. He reminded me of a bass player, constantly seduced by the band's groove.

And then there was Yvon. He was the owner of the Civic, though he never drove it. A hefty fellow, he was constantly the butt of Chris and Trevor's jokes. Had the four of us been walking along the railroad tracks instead of travelling down the 401 towards Detroit, Yvon would have been our Vern Tessio.

I wasn't sure exactly where I fit into this troupe, since I was at a point in my life where I wasn't sure how I fit into anything. Because my passion for the trip was so evident though, I blended in well enough.

As we neared the American border I began to feel comfortable in the company of my troupe, but not comfortable enough to disclose a scandalous yet very relevant piece of information: I was bringing a few joints along for this trip.

I wondered: what rock band worth its skin hadn't done the same? How is a young band without any contacts south of the 49th parallel supposed to smoke a few joints after what may very well be their last show in America? Entrance into the musicians' union should include a clandestine sticker to be placed on the front of the touring van that labels bands as users, not pushers. But the mind begins to wander in the last few minutes and you become caught in a movie where the script is beyond your control.

The Honda pulled to a stop at the border and all four of us assumed the position: silent, clearly nervous, but affable. I've never been sure how border guards distinguish between the genuine fear of getting caught for a crime and the intuitive fear of a uniform. Within this car were both kinds of characters. My palms began to sweat.

"Identification?" asked the border guard, with a sly tone and a slick moustache.

It became tough to keep a grip on the ID in my hand.

"Any of you guilty of a crime for which a pardon has not been granted?"

"No sir."

"You realize if I check these IDs and you're lying, I'm going to have to pull you over and bring you into custody?"

"Yes sir."

Come on man, I was thinking. *We've all jay-walked or smashed something in our time, but just ask what I know you have to.*

"Anyone carrying any illegal drugs or firearms in the car?"

Fuck dude, I thought this was Detroit! If we've got a joint or two, do you really think that's going to sway the violence and drug use that the Western world is assured runs rampant through your city?

Instead of this outburst I sweated out another pound or two. Being asked this question is like being questioned by a lover about your faith in a relationship. Your face becomes so confident that you begin to believe that there aren't five joints in your bag and that she's just a friend.

"No sir."

He looked at each of us and the scene seemed to last an eternity, instead of the few seconds it really was.

"All right, you seem like nice Canadians. Don't let me down. I don't want to see you back here for the wrong reasons."

He stared deep into my eyes. *I'll indulge with moderation,* I thought. But as soon as he waved us through I realized I'd been lying to him.

We were all relieved when we made it through and I was beginning to feel a certain kinship with these dudes. Little did I know, I would soon need any kinship I could get my hands on.

◆◆◆

After a rendezvous with Hugh at the Fox Theatre, we found ourselves at a dank apartment that belonged to a friend of Hugh's on Detroit's notorious Cass Ave. Chris had arranged for us to spend the night there.

The apartment was better suited for vagrants and junkies than four bewildered Canadians who would have called our embassy in a panic if we ever found ourselves lost in this neighbourhood. There were bullet holes in the walls. Cockroaches gave us the once-over as we lugged our pillows and sleeping bags up the rickety elevator. For a middle-class kid raised in suburbia, this was the scariest thing I'd ever done. I wondered how much I really loved this band. It was clear from my companions' pursed lips that we were all thinking the same thing.

Soon, we met the rest of our crew, some more friends

of Hugh's. They ran the gamut of forty-something Hip fans: the hard-drinking auto worker and the daft, denim-clad cougar. The last member of the group was a stocky construction worker whose face constantly wore a confused grin and who never offered more than a few snickers to the conversation. I kept my distance from him the whole night.

We spent the afternoon of the gig assuaging our fears by overindulging in cheap American beer and Hugh's grass. It took a few beers before I found the courage to bring out my own stash, even though we were already in a benign cloud by that point. Hugh laughed heartily at my meagre contribution, diffusing any potential tension with my compatriots. It was just a few hours until the gig. We were now riding the same wave.

But by the time we left for the gig, I could barely stand. In an effort to forget that I'd have to lay my head down in that shithole, I had too many beers and smoked too much of Hugh's finest. It was all I could do to focus on the Sam Roberts Band during their opening set (which is a shame because the spirit and grandeur of the Fox Theatre is a sight to behold). And there I sat alone, slumped in my chair. My crew, having purchased tickets earlier, were a good dozen rows ahead of me. I stood up and tried my damndest to soak up the atmosphere before collapsing into my seat. I had a paralyzing case of the spins.

Of course, The Hip dealt with the Fox Theatre like the pros they are. They have always managed to put the gig first. Their stoic professionalism not only keeps them in business, it's one of the keys to the loyalty their fans have continued to espouse for over twenty years. In an age when bands come and go frequently and flagrantly, The Hip can always be depended on to play every gig like it's their last. What's more, the band showed virtually no signs of opening-night jitters. There is a strange feeling that sweeps through crowds on the opening night of a tour. Fans wait, staring at the stage, curious to see what kind of carnage the band can dream up. It's the theatrical unpredictability of opening night that renders fans helpless. How will the new songs sound? How will the band look? What sort of old gems will they dust off? While great, unimaginable things happen every day, fans like me look forward to the opening night of a tour as if we are the only ones privy to seeing a rocket launch deep into the untamed sky.

The Hip were efficient and unwavering, a well-oiled machine. When they did show a little flair, during the outro to a particularly haunting version of the acoustic "Scared," I stood up and tried yet again to soak it all in. Gord went off on a Bruce Cockburn tune, yodelling to the cheap seats. (In 2004, cheap seats actually *existed.* Twenty bucks American for a show seemed fair, and I can't remember thinking that about any Hip gig since.) And from that outro, the band launched into "As Makeshift As We Are." It was the last thing I remember.

In retrospect, it was appropriate that "As Makeshift As We Are" was the last song I heard that night. I always chuckle when I hear the song now, and the admission Gord delivers:

> "Here's where I slowly close my eyes/And say I'm too drunk for this/Yea, I'm too drunk for this"

Before this trip my hangovers were usually easy to combat, if I even experienced them at all. The following morning's hangover, however, would be the first time I ever felt the appalling waves of self-loathing that I know all too well today, led by my brazen contempt for The Hip's performance.

I was awoken by fans kicking at my legs. Twenty dollars not-so-wisely spent. I'd fallen victim to a cliché: Canadians so excited to see "their band" spending the night in a haze instead of appreciating them.

My troupe and I soon found ourselves back on Cass Ave. The natural post-show buzz disappeared as we walked through the dilapidated building. It brought us closer to the stark realization that what we were doing for The Hip wasn't just "worth it," but commendable. I was quickly brought back down to Earth, however, when Chris hooked his video camera up to the TV to run through a few highlights from the night's gig.

The early stuff felt good to revisit, but pangs of remorse began to creep in. As Chris fast-forwarded his way through the video, Trevor called out: "Hey, we gotta watch 'Three Pistols!' They killed that one tonight!"

I sat there, shivering, and thinking to myself, *Fuck, they played "Three Pistols" tonight?*

It burned like a million rusted razors scraping against my all-too-sensitive skin. But I kept quiet, knowing that if I confessed, I'd lose any credibility I might have established on the trip.

I watched the rest of the highlights in horror. Being the kind of keener who waits outside of venues for hours before the doors open, I knew I'd done myself and the band a disservice. I wasn't a fan, I was a fraud. My allegiance felt strained. My eyes grew heavy. Seeing as how "Three Pistols" had closed the set, we all found spots to lie down and call it a strange night. I curled my sweater into a ball for a pillow and passed out. I had to escape what had happened. Tomorrow would be another day. I resolved to wake with poise. But first, I'd have to make it through the night.

Much has been made of the mythology that surrounds rock and roll: alcohol, drugs, poor personal hygiene, and all manner of youth gone wild. Though they enjoy posh surroundings these days, even The Rolling Stones spent some time in squalid conditions. And while I'm not comparing my plight to that of Mick and Keef, sleeping on that filthy floor was a sacrifice.

All I'd wanted was to see my favourite band on fresh soil. I wondered: does this band know how far their fans will go for rock and roll salvation? What I had failed to notice, though, was the shifty old construction worker passed out beside me. While I slept fitfully with sirens raging outside, he rolled on top of me and started groping my chest. The Gods of Rock and Roll were exacting a timely revenge on me for not being a dedicated fan.

Now, it's possible that my suitor was used to a warm body next to him. Regardless, I tossed him off my chest. I entertained the idea of catching the next Greyhound back to Guelph. I wanted to be anywhere but lying on that cold floor. With a snore he went in for the kill again. I wanted to scream. I muscled him off, this time with anger. But I had nothing against him; I was angry at myself. Being careless around the things you love, especially when you're out of your comfort zone, is about as terrible a sin as a twenty-one-year-old with no criminal inclinations can commit. The truth was staring at me through the dark: I will never remember most of the Detroit gig, but will always associate my time in one of America's great rock and roll cities with a gruff, overweight man and his desire to get to second base.

I leapt up at the first sign of the sun with steadfast resolve. I remembered why I was on this trip in the first place: the band. Drugs and booze were in no short supply back in Guelph. I could indulge to my liking and pass out face down on my neighbour's lawn if I felt so inclined, without missing much.

As irresponsible as I'd been, I had a second chance. I awoke my three compatriots and suggested we hit the road, immediately. They agreed.

We hit the I-75 to Cleveland. No one spoke. The sun attacked the car from every angle. I had no one to blame for the misfortunes of the night before but myself; not the band, not my team, not even my portly assailant. By taking the blame for the evening, I learned a little more about what it takes to be a good fan: focus.

Losing sight of the band can happen. But taking them for granted is another thing. I was lucky to be in that car with another gig on the horizon. I couldn't guarantee that I wouldn't get drunk or stoned again, but I had established some limits. The only thing that had room to grow was my appreciation of the band and the responsibility I had to myself.

◆◆◆

A discussion of the greatest rock and roll frontmen of all time will inevitably lead to names like Jagger, Morrison, Tyler, and Daltrey. If everyone's had a few drinks, you might see someone's peacock strut, hear a feminine wail, or watch a make-believe microphone get tossed around. (Hopefully not with a beer bottle in place of a microphone, I can attest that no good will come of this.)

While including Gord Downie in that lineup might seem like a stretch, it's no dig on his onstage persona. He may not have the worldwide recognition, but Downie's affect as a frontman is a little more personal and a lot more regional. Downie's legacy as a performer is just as permanent as those two Brits and two Yanks, it's just a matter of who you ask.

From the moment Downie walks onstage, the crowd is his drug. Every song in The Hip's repertoire renders him a performer possessed and leaves fans captivated.

Downie is a constant artist. There's the free-form poetry that he adds to every musical break, often testing out new lyrics. There's the interpretive dancing that Rob's expansive solos inspire. He paints the crowd with his microphone, mimics a gorilla and eats the hair of those in the front row.

The manner in which he floats upon the collective energy between the stage and the crowd seems effortless.

Yet Downie's knock-out punch is the way he can harness a moment and drag everyone around him into his beautiful, transcendental world and make them feel welcome. Yes, many laugh in confusion the first time they see him onstage but ultimately it's tough not to fall under his spell. CBC weatherwoman and old friend Johanna Wagstaffe, for one, shouted at me during her first show, as Downie stomped around the stage during a raging "Gus: The Polar Bear From Central Park," and pierced the first few rows with his pensive stare: "It's like he's staring into our souls."

He may be a freak, but to fans of the band, he's *our* freak. His onstage persona represents the struggle between impassioned artistic nobility, which fans of The Hip respect, and wide-scale commercial success, which has long eluded the band. Anyone who's seen Downie live can knock off a Downie impersonation, whether decent or laughable. Even before I saw The Hip live, my Downie impersonation was top-notch thanks to traded, poorly recorded VHS concerts. Before YouTube, this was how obsessed fans got their rocks off.

I'd stand on my bed, watching these tapes while emulating his every twist, wag, and wander. How he continually found new meaning in the same songs every night was a constant source of fascination. The "Poets" from the July 24th, 1998 show at Wetlands Preserve in New York City was nothing like the "Poets" from the 9:30 Club in Washington on July 30th, 2002. When I'd talk about The Hip with friends, it seemed like I was the only one who understood the magnitude of this. That was until Uncle Mike (of *Fully Completely* cassette fame) busted in on me dancing like a lunatic while my parents hosted a dinner party upstairs. He never publicly embarrassed me for my bedroom star worship, so I figured I owed him.

In the fall of 2002, during my first year of university, The Hip announced two New Years' Eve shows in Hamilton. Convinced that something epic would happen on New Years' Eve (when you're eighteen, this is a common belief), I only bought tickets for the December 30th show. Deciding who to take to the show wasn't much of an issue. Everyone I knew at university was already sick of The Hip, as I'd been overplaying them during my first month in residence and I'd already booked shows in October with some hometown buddies for the band's two-night stand at Toronto's Hummingbird Centre. This left me with only one option: my "Favourite Uncle" (still one of the coolest titles available for grown men).

Sure, as an eighteen-year-old trying to find his social footing in university, I was taking a chance by inviting him. But I was sick of trying to convert people. I needed a bona fide fan and the comfort of an open and encouraging ear.

The ride from my hometown of Oshawa to Hamilton was an exercise in how to get psyched for a gig. I gabbed on about The Hip and Uncle Mike listened earnestly. The smile on his face grew with every kilometre. In order to throw your weight behind something you love and hope to be successful, you need the full support of your family. Families push you to do better and to take risks in the strangest of ways.

We found a dodgy bar and ordered a few greasy burgers. Feeling liberated and slightly inebriated, I posed a question, though I already knew the answer: "Hey, Uncle Mike. Do you want to go to the Hilton hotel? There's a Hip tribute band doing an early set."

He wore the smile of a child at Christmas. For him, what was happening tonight was already special enough and any addition to the evening was just icing on the cake. For once, I wasn't leading the charge. I found myself feeding off his energy. Here was someone to whom I could express my love for The Hip without the standard roll of the eyes.

The hotel bar was packed, with Hamilton's local modern-rock radio station broadcasting side-stage. As we dove into our pints a DJ welcomed The Practically Hip, one of The Hip's best tribute bands. Though tribute bands can sound rudimentary at times, The Practically Hip (or any good tribute band) can be entertaining if you're in the right mood and give yourself to the moment. My uncle and I were in that moment.

"So before we welcome out The Practically Hip," bellowed the DJ. "I just want to remind you guys again of the contest we've got going on tonight."

Contest?

"During the third song of The Practically Hip's set, you're all welcome to come on the dance floor and perform your best Gord Downie impression. Whoever does the best impression will not only win tickets to tomorrow's New Years' Eve show, but also a night's stay in the Hilton."

It's very easy to remember how I felt when I heard these words because time ceased to exist. I was going to enter and win this contest. Making a fool of myself, especially in front of crowds, wasn't anything new. But those had been crowds of friends I could laugh with later. Getting on stage in front of strangers had me confronting the kind of intense showmanship that I'd long admired in Downie.

A couple of songs later, The Practically Hip launched into "Twist My Arm" and the DJ reappeared. "Okay guys. Here's your chance. Have some fun and let's see what you got!"

I didn't even look at Uncle Mike as I downed my pint and rushed the stage. On the dance floor, a handful of older women were wiggling mildly. No one was doing Downie's charisma any justice. So I broke the rules and hopped onto the stage beside Dean, the lead singer in all his bald-headed glory. He shot me a confused gaze. I was onstage and the crowd was a blur. The only thing I could see clearly was Uncle Mike's wide-open jaw. I was a lion let out of his cage for the first time in years. I danced with the fervour of a young man who'd lost his virginity to a girl way out of his league. I mimicked with the studious passion of the greatest admirer Gord Downie has ever known. I compacted all of his moves into what felt like hours.

Thirty seconds in, the DJ put his hand on my bony shoulder. I thought I was done for. Ejected due to exuberance.

"You can come offstage, man. You've already won!" he shouted in my ear.

I rushed to my uncle. He had to be helped up off the floor. Not from over-indulgence, but laughter.

Somehow I'd completely sobered up from the pints but was now riding an entirely new high. I got a few congratulatory handshakes from the ladies on the dance floor and felt like a hero. But the look in Uncle Mike's eyes made me realize that I couldn't have done it without him. His support had propelled me to the stage. I wanted to impress him almost as much as I wanted the free tickets. We laughed, drank some more pints, then laughed some more. Uncle Mike let me bask in my own glow until show time. And though I'd danced in front of a hundred people or so, it was a story that only the two of us could share.

To this day he will tease me about that evening in front of anyone who will listen. But we share a common understanding. We needed each other that night; he needed my youthful spirit and I needed his paternal encouragement.

The show itself was a banger. Every time Downie busted out a move that I'd tried onstage, we'd explode in simultaneous laughter. Uncle Mike turned out to be one of the best concert buddies I'd ever take in a Hip show with, but not because he bought every burger and every pint and drove me there and back. He reminded me that no matter what risks you take, without the support of those around you, you're nothing more than a fool with a foolish dream.

RISKY MOVES WITHIN THE HIP'S REPERTOIRE

Because of The Hip's tendency to be played to death on classic-rock radio, most casual fans will inevitably identify with their better-known songs. Yet a back catalogue as large as theirs demands consideration.

Bands play their hits live to get a rise out of casual fans. The demands of touring are just that plain. There is, however, a reward for bands that go out on a limb, moving in their own direction artistically, free of restrictions. For everyone who has heard and hated "New Orleans is Sinking," there is a hardcore fan that loves and recognizes the untamed beauty of "Let's Stay Engaged."

The Hip have long had a sound uniquely their own. But it's the songs that the general population might not know that speak the loudest to The Hip's originality. By taking risks and enabling a bit of artistic faith and evolution, these are the tracks that keep hardcore fans warm at night.

Here, for your reading (and hopefully, listening) pleasure are three tracks that casual fans might have missed. These may not be The Hip's best tunes, but they have made their sonic language that much more potent.

"The Last of the Unplucked Gems"
Road Apples
1991

While the bluesy swagger of arena-rockers like "Blow at High Dough" and "New Orleans is Sinking" from their debut full-length *Up To Here* broke The Hip, *Road Apples* solidified the band's presence on the Canadian rock stage. Adopting a southern, gutsy feel, the record owes at least part of its atmosphere to having been recorded in the French Quarter of New Orleans.

At times during *Road Apples*, it's easy to picture the band on a small stage, sweating buckets with dozens of drunken patrons. In the face of the grunge movement that was making quick work of all other cousins of rock and roll, the band managed to carve their own niche. It was defiant bar rock for people who liked to hang out in bars. And after the complicated and processed rock aesthetic of the '80s, The Hip were a simple and healthy alternative.

Lyrics like "Two-fifty for a high ball/And a buck-and-a-half for a beer" may have emphasized the band's collective sound at the time, but the difference between The Hip in 1991 and The Hip a decade later is far from marginal. Many fans have rejected the "New Hip," believing the literary rock that the band has taken to is a betrayal of their roots.

Though the steps were small, there were inroads made by the band from *Up To Here* to *Road Apples.* In terms of lyrical depth and ensuring their potent live show was captured on record, there's a noticeable evolution. However, if the record isn't cranked (though to be fair, it often is) to the highest volume, then the album closer on *Road Apples* can slip by almost unheard.

The subtle, slow-moving groove of "Gems" bears no immediate similarities to the rest of *Road Apples*. The entire pace of the record slows to a crawl. Tracks like "On the Verge" and "Twist My Arm," feature a visceral, dual-guitar attack worthy of your sloppiest dance moves. "The Last of the Unplucked Gems," however, is a two-minute rhythmic jam that showcases, for the first time, the poetic side of the band. It was this poetic side that would ultimately fuel their creative fire for the next ten years:

> "When the mystique varies thus/You can send a man to bury us/It's hard to say, it's sad but true/I'm kinda dumb and so are you"

Finally, they were letting their guard down and showing an eloquent, yet self-deprecating side.

There is nothing that "rocks" about this song. If anything, it should have served as a warning for fans who wanted a generic southern rock band. Since the release of *Road Apples,* The Hip have managed to push their artistic boundaries with every release. "Gems" showed signs of the band they wanted to become.

Soon, brooding jams full of insightful and interpretative lyrics would become such an important part of The Hip's repertoire that fans would clamour for these tracks at concerts as a means to breathe and slowly take in the hundreds or thousands of fans around them. Every band worth its salt needs tracks for fans to raise lighters to and "Gems" was one of The Hip's first.

In 2002, eleven years after the release of *Road Apples,* The Hip were touring intimate theatres for the first time. The band's subtleties reached audiences clearly. It was an experiment; standard Hip songs found new life in new venues. I caught two of these nights at the Hummingbird Centre in Toronto. Both were full of tracks that managed to expand sonically with the new setting. The poetry within The Hip's songs wasn't just audible, it was speaking directly to the crowd.

On the first night, the thick bass line that starts "The Last of the Unplucked Gems" brought forth a wave of applause from a crowd that likely hadn't heard the song in years. The two minutes swept over the audience. As the song drew to a close, the bass line continued. Fans sat on their hands with anticipation, wondering just how long the band was going to let this song wander before moving on to a real banger. Paul's guitar hinted at a seafaring rhythm. It was "The Dire Wolf," one of the better tunes from 2002's *In Violet Light* and one of the most poetic numbers the band has ever recorded. The segue was long and drawn out, but when the tunes finally did merge the crowd fell under the spell. Judging by the smiles around me, they were captivated for good. The Hip linked the old and the new, using their unique voice to speak to the crowd. It may have taken eleven years, but the entire Hummingbird Centre was listening, loud and clear.

"Grace, too"
Day for Night
1994

Summer is the season Canadian music fans live for. Large outdoor festivals provide a respite from the harsh drudgery of winter. And The Hip are always there, providing the voice of salvation. Between 1989 and 2009, there was only one summer when the band did not play a large outdoor venue.

The summer before *Day for Night* was released, The Hip began their inaugural "Another Roadside Attraction" tour. An array of touring acts, headlined by The Hip, highlighted a full day's worth of music. The benign, jovial sounds of The Hip's three previous albums fell upon ears that had been waiting for them all winter. These three releases were so joyous and upbeat that The Hip quickly became the de facto band of choice for Canadian summer barbecues. The nature of The Hip's early work is so communal that fans forget the harsh realities of winter as soon as the rising chorus of "Courage" from *Fully Completely* takes hold.

Fully Completely is one of the quintessential Canadian records of the '90s. It's a bright listen; radio-ready tracks and a sense of geographic exploration abound. Sonically, the band is concise, their chunky rhythms now fully realized. When Hip fans were asked to vote for their favourite tracks to make up the appropriately titled *Yer Favourites*, a contractually obligated Greatest Hits album, seven of the album's twelve cuts were voted in.

A couple of years after the release of *Fully Completely*, Kurt Cobain took grunge to the grave and Woodstock '94 brought a variety of genres to the masses, all available for consumption on television. Whereas the early '90s had provided a sense of promise and purpose for rock and roll, half a decade in, rock and roll as it were, was looking for a place to happen.

Canadian rock fans looking for some reliability turned to The Hip. The band was set to release *Day for Night* in September of 1994. What else could confirm that there was no cause for alarm in the world of rock and roll but some classic Hip, as meaty and pure as the steaks and burgers fans would barbecue in accompaniment to the first spin of the record?

Instead, *Day for Night* exalted the unenviable lows of Canadian seasons, painting an accurately bleak portrait of winter. The Hip had managed to explore the depths of the Canadian psyche just as their fans were looking for an escape from those very lows.

The Hip had created their "dark" record. There was nothing immediately redeeming on *Day for Night.* Even the album's standout track, "Nautical Disaster," tells the tale of thousands of people dying in a shipwreck off the coast of France. With the world of rock open and ready for The Hip's taking, another album full of feel-good jams could have pushed them into the American mainstream. Instead, they went introspective. The Hip sang of destitution and questioned everything around them. With intense, concentrated lyrics like "If there's glory in miracles/It's that they're reversible" from "Titanic Terrarium" they ruminated on their very existence.

Hearing the album's opener, "Grace, too," against previous booming and festive lead-off tracks like "Little Bones" and "Courage" probably had fans wondering: had this band devolved into a Depeche Mode rip-off band? Beginning with looping drums, the song gives way to an intoxicating bass line, followed by a penetrating riff. The vibe is a dank basement full of pot smoke. Gord's vocals are distant, as if he is chanting through rain, calling out to anyone who can hear him. His pitch is strained and paranoid. Before the song busts out into a minute-and-a-half-long jam that ends the track, Gord shouts nonsensically in a newfound warble, pleading with listeners to engage in the darker edges of their subconscious.

"Grace, too" was the band's first attempt at anything remotely psychedelic. The first time I fell victim to a few too many joints and the waves of paranoia clicked in, I retreated into my bedroom and listened to "Grace, too" in the dark. The track's stewing stomp was strangely comforting.

A few summers before that harsh winter evening I spent freaking out, The Hip played Woodstock '99. Out of shear obligation I tuned in to my first Pay Per View event. They opened the Saturday of the event, not a spot to be taken lightly.

The band strolled onstage just after noon, to a sea of Canadian flags and a deafening audience. The sun beat down on the crowd. This was the band that the Canadians in attendance had come to see. And what better way to reward the dehydrated masses of dedicated fans than with a set of upbeat tracks?

The Hip opened with "Grace, too." The crowd instinctively became elated and rose with the song's climb. Through five years of touring the song, it had evolved into a sprawling, feel-good track. The band had managed to imbue the charm of the past four Canadian summers into a track which, when first released, rallied against everything summer stood for.

Sure, they had taken a chance by releasing a darker record. But even after taking this chance, The Hip allowed the lead-off track to grow with a sense of buoyancy. "Grace, too," for everything it can encompass, will always be my favourite Hip song.

Though certain tracks have specific connotations, it is the job of an obsessed fan to allow these songs to grow. Pigeonholing songs is for casual fans; obsessed fans hear possibilities and interpretations when others do not. The first time I heard "Grace, too," it scared the shit out of me. (Though, I was eleven at the time. Vegetables and dogs made me wet my pants as well.) Just six years later, a live version of "Grace, too" was the first track I ever played while driving with the windows down. Faith in a band's vision, even if it means going alone and against the grain is what separates the obsessed from the masses.

The Hip went to a forbidden place with the studio version of "Grace, too." Now, to hear it at a summer gig and *not* shed your skin in an act of liberation is forbidden. The song still wanders, but now with a smile on its face.

"Family Band"
World Container
2006

Having followed the band's career for thirteen years by the release of *World Container*, I'd had moments of frustration with their output. Though the inspiration they provided was never in short supply, in the latter of those thirteen years the number of times I wondered if I'd be able to truly understand what drove The Hip began to rival the inspiration. I was a fan who couldn't just skim the details, but there was still so much beyond my grasp. There was still a theoretical door that the band wouldn't open for me.

The first time I heard "Family Band," I was sitting in a cramped university library cubicle. In the thick of midterms, like many students I took advantage of every distraction on offer. The band had begun streaming the yet-to-be-released

World Container on their website. Any chance of me passing the next day's midterm disappeared.

As my enthusiasm turned into giddiness, I fell victim to the pop-song attention span; I clicked "next" every two-and-a-half minutes, whether the song was finished or not. I couldn't sit still. My mind was working overtime.

That was until the tenth track, "Family Band," which I played half a dozen times in succession. Unlike some immediate Hip classics, "Family Band" didn't jump into the upper echelon of the Hip canon right away. But with its affectionate, swirling undertones and Downie's determined voice begging not just to be heard, but *listened* to, the song became impossible to turn away from. After a few years of frustration from a lack of understanding, the song had me intrigued and dumbfounded all the same.

I spent the next few months grappling with "Family Band." But for me it was still nothing more than the tightest track on *World Container.*

Those months after *World Container* was released were the most mundane of my life. I was back at university after a year teaching overseas. I couldn't stand being on the other side of the classroom and was desperate for new revelations. I turned to those close to me but no one could help me shake the rut I was wallowing in. I welcomed 2007 with little hope.

The Hip began one of their famous winter tours across Canada seven days into 2007. At the very least, I thought The Hip could be counted on to provide me with some truth, even if the lines of communication had been strained of late.

My father caught the band's show in Barrie on the 25th of January. I would see the band in my hometown a week later. I told him to keep notes. To make matters more intense, he was heading to the gig with an entourage of Klokes: his two brothers and my cousin, who was taking in his first

Hip show. The afternoon of the gig, I began to sweat. I wondered if my sixteen-year-old cousin would be inspired enough by the band's live set to continue carrying the torch. Fans don't just worry about how the band's music will affect them, but those close to them as well. In turn, they look to those people to reinforce their belief in the band if ever they should waver. Being a fan is indeed, a full-time job.

The next day my father relayed his thoughts on the gig. While the entire clan of Kloke men were blown away, one particular anecdote caught my attention. After a legendary rendition of The Clash's "Train in Vain," The Hip treated fans to a raucous "Family Band." With lyrics both cryptic ("I can't smell a rat when it's all rat/I can't find one in an elevator/My mind doesn't work so bad/But I am a poor exterminator") and heartbreakingly honest ("One day I'll make some honest rock and roll/Full of hand claps and gang vocals/I'm gonna get all the children involved/We're gonna get lost on all you locals") it's understandable that the Klokes would have been a little lost. They turned to my father for guidance, figuring the oldest of the bunch would be able to decipher Gord's message.

"I told them it was about exterminators and all the rats among us," he said in a serious tone.

I chuckled. "Do you really think that's what the song is about?" I asked, genuinely curious.

"Josh, how the hell would I know?" he laughed. It was one of the first times my father, the infinite source of wisdom, had ever admitted that the truth was beyond his grasp.

After our conversation, I retreated to my headphones to listen to "Family Band" yet again. My father's honesty led me to realize that often, the truth isn't something one has to search for, sometimes it presents itself. For the past thirteen years I had been searching for hidden meanings in each and every Hip track to apply to my own life. And now, it was clear.

"Family Band" was The Hip's way of telling their fans who they were. They had worked hard, but only continued because of the people around them. The relationship between a band and its followers is not unlike the relationship between parents and children. They give, and we take. But at a certain age, it's possible for everyone to loosen up and show their true selves. The Hip had created a family; each and every one of their fans was part of that family. Worldwide success had always eluded the band, yet no level of success could ever take away from the personal relationships they'd formed with their fans. Families are never chosen but to a fan, the cryptic lyrics in "Family Band" were The Hip's way of saying they were happy with the cards they'd been dealt:

> "We'll be a shade shy of true wickedness/We'll be a shade shy of truly loving this, yeah/There are other things we'd rather be doing, sure/Even nothing with you"

I couldn't help but become a slave to the song that night under the headphones. My eyes welled up. The band had bared themselves for everyone around them. The next time I saw my cousin I picked his brain like a psychologist. A year-and-a-half later, another cousin saw the band live for the first time. It had taken me thirteen years to see the band in a different, more truthful light. I hoped that it wouldn't take my cousin and the rest of my family as long to realize the truth that could stare them in the face in the dead of winter, on a stage, together with everyone that mattered to them.

"We've opened for [The Tragically Hip] over 80 times now. We'd been around but we were still a pretty inexperienced band going into it. We came out of that tour in 2004 having learned probably the most important lesson you're going to learn as a musician who is going to get up onstage and that's to never mail it in. Never give any less than all of yourself. I've watched them do it night after night and tried to absorb that lesson into how we play and it still resonates with me all these years later. It's never enough. You can never give enough of yourself. I learnt that from them."

— *Sam Roberts,* What It's Like to Tour With The Tragically Hip, *The Toronto Star, Friday, July 22, 2016*

CHAPTER 4

Attach Emotions to Songs

I've had many an argument about the pop artists who dominate the video and airwaves and their lack of merit. While I try to be fair, I get suspicious whenever I hear names like Bieber and Gaga. The very essence of pop music is temporary and replaceable. These acts may sing and dance, but they're nothing more than a McDonald's burger: immediately satisfying with no long-term benefits. A pop star's song isn't being sold so much as their image is. It's hard to imagine a Justin Bieber song without picturing his shiny face.

True songs don't need a video accompaniment. They are stories that are crafted from a place impossible to find on a map, where the salt of the earth crashes against the inescapable human condition; where the stories are bigger than the storytellers.

Hip songs can capture, and then bottle, raw emotion. When I hear a song, I'm brought back to the exact moment when it latched itself onto my subconscious. Often, these songs bring forth a rush of emotion that is both temporarily displacing and incredibly reassuring.

◆◆◆

As a kid, I tried to push the boundaries, if only slightly. Every day of my youth I warmed to the notion that there was a world outside of the sheltered suburban one that revolved primarily around my best friend's basement and weekly soccer practices. While the familiarity of The Hip contributed to the comfort that kept me close to home for so long, it was the subtle yearning within "Locked in the Trunk of a Car," or the wandering rumble of "Chagrin Falls," that encouraged me to keep my ears and eyes open.

And when I decided to get the hell out of dodge, The Hip helped me begin three important journeys by virtue of the random beauty that was once rock radio. Now, I cannot hear these songs without remembering that I actually followed through on each journey.

In high school, I had a big mouth that got me into, and subsequently out of, trouble. My teachers got wise by the time I graduated, but early on a guidance counsellor decided to pop the bubble that had grown around my head and give me a taste of the world outside of my hometown of Oshawa. I was to be shipped off on a train to Ottawa, alone, for a national leadership camp that would teach me how to use my big mouth. In meeting student leaders from across the country, I was supposed to realize that I was just a big fish in a small pond.

Like any teenager who runs his mouth, I wasn't half as confident as I let on. The thought of actually leaving my comfort zone had me dripping with sweat. I began to worry that my loud-mouth approach wouldn't work with people who hadn't grown up with me.

It was the first trip I'd ever taken alone. I had nightmares of making a lousy first impression and then spending the remaining days wallowing in homesickness. All of this before I had even left the house.

As my family drove me to the train station, my father turned the radio up. "Last American Exit" was playing, one of The Hip's few strong tracks from their self-titled debut

EP. There is an unmitigated poise in the song. Long, drawn-out guitar solos coupled with the band's young, carefree groove served as perfect departure music. While I wasn't heading to America, I knew I didn't have to be nervous anymore because I had something tangible that wasn't wrought with overconfidence.

During those five days, I became known as "the guy who likes The Hip" thanks to bombastic displays of fandom and constantly using the band a means to start conversation. It was my attempt to show everyone that I wasn't just a scared shithead. In doing so, I showed who I really was: a fan. For the first time, I had nothing to hide.

◆◆◆

I wasn't crazy about heading to university. I don't think most young men are. The sexual food chain for younger men is built upon age; through the first few years of high school, boys realize that girls their own age only really show interest in older men. We (the young men, the literal hunters on this food chain) wait for the last year or two of high school to finally get a bit of vindication, only to be shipped off to university where we enter at the bottom of the ladder again.

I didn't say much on the hour-and-a-half drive from my home in Oshawa to the University of Guelph. Overcome with awkward anticipation, I wasn't ready to be diving into the next four years. (Does pretending to be asleep constitute the proper beginning to the "best years of your life?") We pulled off the mighty Highway 401 onto Highway 6 and traffic slowed to a standstill. Around me, thousands of kids were about to enter the great unknown, with dreams of keg stands and random fornication and somehow, coming out at the other end with a piece of paper. I was told by my better teachers in my last days of high school that only half of students who enter university actually finish. I was worried about making it through the first day. I had nothing to fall back on except myself, and that wasn't an encouraging prospect.

Overzealous volunteers directed us towards the campus. Their enthusiasm made me sick. Clearly, they'd survived. They'd found a will and a way. Wide awake now, my younger sister sensed my feelings of dread.

"How you doing?" she asked with a smirk.

"Shut up," I said.

This, the height of our communication.

Many of the volunteers were advertising CFRU 93.3, the school's radio station. My father, gung ho as he was, wanted to fall in line. He fiddled with the radio dial. I felt like telling him to fuck off. Where I wanted to be, there were no radio dials. Just a comfort zone I knew I'd never see again.

The DJ was welcoming students with pride as if to say, you're one of us now. But I didn't want to be part of his club. He played ten minutes of unlistenable tribal noise-rock far removed from anything I'd ever heard before, only validating my opinion.

Our van was lifeless. We were so close to the campus now that I felt I needed to accept my fate. Without warning, the DJ dropped "Courage" on us, a seminal Hip track full of determined zeal and presence. The riff sent waves of purpose rippling through my veins.

> "Courage/My word/It didn't come, it doesn't matter/
> Courage/My word/It couldn't come at a worse time."

How quickly a young man likens his plight to disaster and forgets that everywhere, at any time, people are facing real problems. "Courage," in all its pulsating glory, made me realize that I had a world of opportunity in front of me, if only I could muster up a little bravado. The whole van chuckled while I tapped my toes to Johnny Fay's reliable and unrelenting drum work. The song gave my body a pulse again. I was still scared, but at least I remembered that The Hip could get me out of these jams. The song ended with its timely, blissful fade out and we pulled into the campus. Not a month later, I'd get a note on the erasable marker board on the front of my dorm room:

"Dear Josh. Enough is enough. Please, stop playing The Hip."

◆◆◆

After that first year, friends recognized that I was joined at the hip (!) to my favourite band and had become numb to my obsession. But during my continued traipsing through dozens of concerts in Canada and the States, my mind began to wander.

Sick of only reading about places in classes that bored me to death, by my third year I was entertaining the idea of leaving. The next thing I knew, I was sitting alone in my childhood bedroom one early evening, sweating the fact that I was about to tell my parents over a home-cooked meal that I wanted to leave university with just one year to go and teach English abroad to discover a planet I'd only read about.

Once again, my sister joined me: "You know what you're going to say then?"

"I think so."

Needless to say, our relationship had evolved.

As I tucked my last bits of salmon tortellini away, I dropped the bomb. My parents, supportive as they were, asked me if I was running away from something.

"No, I think I'm running towards something."

"You think you'll be able to handle a year alone on the other side of the world?"

"Yes, I do."

I'll always remember my father, scribbling notes on his

napkin (as Kloke males are prone to do). When I gave him my answer, he scribbled one word in bold letters:

COURAGE

Eight months later I awoke to a life-altering day. I had two suitcases packed at the front door and was about to head to Pearson International Airport for a one-way flight to Warsaw, Poland.

My father turned the radio to Q107, Toronto's classic rock station, as soon as we hit the highway. Led Zeppelin's "Out on the Tiles" was playing as I stared out the window with a sly grin on my face. I thought about the person I could become, thousands of kilometres away from home. Pensive? Aggressive? Hopeless? I had begun a search that would last a year. I knew once I got on that plane, I'd be able to change for the better (or worse) without anyone to answer to; an emotional blank slate.

A brief pause hit the airwaves. If the DJ decided to play "Don't Stop Believin'" I probably never would have come back. If "Go Your Own Way" was spun we all would have cracked up simultaneously, if only to break the tension. And if the DJ had played "Bad 'N' Ruin" then my homecoming, tail between my legs, probably would have been assured before I'd even left. But instead, the DJ gave me the push on the swing I needed. The DJ gave me the groove of "Grace, too."

My sister was the first to realize. She laughed, punched me in the arm and screamed, "Oh my fucking god!"

She screamed to point out the obvious: if anything was to be done this year, it might as well be done with the sense of freedom the song had always brought me. As we sped down the 401, I felt every care and responsibility I once believed to be important disappear. We hadn't even reached the airport and I was weightless. Those pulsating bass lines

I'd danced to had shown me how to actually move.

Once my parents and I had our requisite teary good-byes, I did three things: called a few friends from a pay-phone one last time, smiled because I was actually doing something of consequence and along the moving walkways, with head (and headphones) held high, I danced. I didn't have to answer to anyone.

Growing up in the suburbs and pining to get out was one cliché, but actually leaving was another cliché altogether. The lift-off and altitude sent a rush of blood to my head. The plane left the safe, comfortable earth of Canada and took a hard right.

◆◆◆

Not every departure we make in life is geographical. While bands make sonic transitions from album to album, fans mimic these transitions in their own lives as well. There are songs within The Hip's catalogue that, in turn, do not represent a departure from one place on the Earth to another, but instead from one stage of my life to another.

Above gentle acoustic guitars, "Bobcaygeon" tells the story of a cop falling in love. The loose rhythm borders on country music. Bobcaygeon, a simple, rustic cottage town, is juxtaposed with a line about a "night in Toronto." Fans from Toronto, not surprisingly, go apeshit when it's played live.

What was once a simple, catchy, head-nodding acoustic track grew in epic proportions for me during the first of the band's two nights at the Molson Amphitheatre in early August, 2002. The night found me in attendance with an unlikely array of friends: an old work acquaintance, a friend from a soccer team and another from high school that I'd only known for a year or so. We all got drunk on the three or four beers it took back then. This was me, trying to branch out before leaving for university in a few weeks.

Throughout that summer, I'd been trying on a few different outfits, both literally and emotionally. I thought I'd need a new persona to survive in university. Somehow, that idea translated into wearing a cowboy hat, something I'd never done before, to this gig.

I looked like an idiot, parading around drunk at the show with the obnoxious hat. As much as I tried to establish my new persona though, nothing could tear me away from the band when they hit the stage. Through the first four songs of the night, including raging versions of "New Orleans is Sinking" and "Fully Completely," I danced with abandon as I always had.

With the hat now bringing added attention, a curly-haired vixen approached and told me how much she and her friends had enjoyed my additions to The Hip's performance from a few rows back. This new guise seemed to be working. It didn't take long for us to begin making out.

Now, I'm not averse to public displays of affection. But when we began rounding second base and heading into third, in plain view of the entire lawn section of the Amphitheatre, I realized this was a little more risqué than my previous forays with girls. I suppose I have the hat and The Hip to thank. The whole time, the band was serenading us with the sweet sounds of "Bobcaygeon."

As the song reached its end, her conscience got the best of her. She disappeared, never giving me her name. I was left with only a story to tell (thankfully one of my buddies caught a glimpse, for posterity's sake), and the memory of a song that I had never really been fond of.

"Bobcaygeon" represented a massive shift for The Hip. It won them a Juno for "Best Single," one of their last major awards. "Bobcaygeon" stretches across genres, finding a home on classic rock, modern rock, country, and adult contemporary radio stations.

The Hip's decline in wide-scale popularity after "Bobcaygeon" can be attributed to a number of factors: they were beginning to age, and middle-aged men don't sell records based on their looks. And after 1998's *Phantom Power*, where "Bobcaygeon" finds a home, The Hip took giant artistic leaps, making their two most eclectic and inaccessible records.

The band created a divide in the early 2000s. A lack of catchy hit singles didn't win them many new fans, but the artistic risks they took after "Bobcaygeon" helped to solidify their existing fanbase. Those who had stuck with The Hip not only respected these changes but also revelled in the chance to support the band while the mainstream turned its back.

◆◆◆

Your teenage years can be a harrowing time. Choosing to align yourself with a group of people you've never met can be nerve-wracking too. But as you age, your musical tastes are subjected less and less to the criticism of your peers. Even in high school, I was aligning myself with a band that aesthetically seemed to have more in common with my father than with me.

But that's ultimately why I stuck with them. The band has rolled with the punches and continued to forge ahead with their artistic vision.

I am ashamed of past behaviour, yet dry-humping a girl in a crowd of twenty thousand is a story I will gladly share in a heartbeat. Likewise, "Bobcaygeon" is a story that The Hip can share with an entire country of both casual fans and diehards alike.

The song will always represent a division for me between the flawed teenager I was, who fell in love with this band and wore their colours on his sleeve with a sense of patriotism, and the man I thought I could become, who assumed maturity occurs without any effort. What's more, it represents a division in the band's career, between being the musical darlings of a country, and a band that was slowly fading into obscurity simply because they wanted to keep doing what they loved.

"I would definitely credit [Plaskett's opening slot on The Tragically Hip's 2004 tour] with upping my awareness of how to play to a large room. Watching Gord do that, you know, he had things he'd do every night on that tour. He'd do a thing with his handkerchief, he'd wrestle his microphone and I wrestle my microphone nightly in my own show now and that may be partly influenced by touring with them. It's always been something I've wrestled with anyway but when you see him, the thing I love about what he does, being on tour with him and watching him nightly, there was a freedom in what he did. There were things he'd do every night but then there were times when he'd go further. Further into whatever was in his brain. It's liberating to know that your audience is there for you. And watching them, I realized that Gord has a real understanding of that. Where he can say, 'Well, why wouldn't I take a risk? Why wouldn't I be myself? These people want that.' What brings you back to a show again and again? Something further. It was freeing to watch him be himself and go beyond himself. He's a reserved guy in many respects but onstage he would just do his thing. It was really playful. It was a beautiful thing to watch. They have serious songs and they have playful songs. That juxtaposition is something I aspire to in my own songs."

— *Joel Plaskett*

CHAPTER 5

You're in this Thing Alone

People who meet obsessed fans like me assume that not only do I share my love of The Hip indiscriminately, but when I meet another fan of the band, that I share my experiences instantaneously. Unfortunately for prospective matchmakers, this couldn't be further from the truth.

Since that first track I heard in the summer of 1993, my relationship with the band has grown from casual fandom to obsession. Though I've been reluctant to admit it over the years, the relationship music fans have with their bands can be religious in nature. We have accepted a doctrine of principles (usually the band's influences and their place in the music world, be it indie darling, stadium giant, or in The Hip's case, a complexity dependent on geography), a gathering place (anywhere the tour bus parks itself), a cast of characters with specific roles (disgruntled drummers who left the band, overzealous rockers who gave in to temptation, stern guitarists who act as the band's emotional anchor, and frontmen who fans worship with unwavering passion), and finally, the highs and lows of their career, with which fans can usually personally identify. Everyone who reads the Bible has a favourite passage; everyone who loves a band has a favourite song or lyric. Everyone who reads the Bible has done so in a time of need; everyone has used their favourite band as a crutch.

Often fans cannot properly explain why they would leave in the middle of a university exam to buy concert tickets the moment they go on sale (still managed a D+ in 19th Century European History) or would go to a gig alone. The very notion of riding solo at a concert reeks of lunacy to most.

For obsessed fans, the connection at gigs is a spiritual one. It's not something we brag about, or even speak about openly. Hip fans were increasingly forced to attend gigs alone at the turn of the century, as the band's mass popularity began to wane and there were fewer radio-ready songs to sing along to. What's more, as the band got older, their need for comfort on the road increased. Ticket prices rose—somewhat predictably. Playing for peanuts and living out of a cramped van in your twenties is one thing, but when you're trying to balance a family life with being on the road for extended periods of time, through my rose-coloured eyes, this rise in price was justified. But how could I continue to ask friends, who were only casual fans, to shell out more than fifty dollars to see a band that had, in their eyes, stopped making good records years before?

Hip fans have always subscribed to a mantra that gives us comfort: "It'd be better for me if you don't understand." It's a telling lyric from 1992's "Locked in the Trunk of a Car." People are scared of what they don't understand, but those whose fandom runs deep relish being inside that trunk while, in their minds at least, the rest of the world stands wondering what's happening inside of it.

◆◆◆

Fans feel guilty when their band is playing within driving distance and they don't attend the gig. I'd snuck out of the aforementioned exam to buy tickets to The Hip's gig in

London, Ontario on November 27th, 2004 but didn't buy tickets for the night before at the Air Canada Centre in Toronto. Perhaps snagging fourth row seats for the London gig assuaged some of my pain. But three days before the ACC gig, I sat staring at my computer. Members of The Hip's message board were offering up single tickets at face value (fans look out for each other that way).

With barely enough cash, I bought a ticket. The afternoon of the gig, I snuck out of my shabby university house when no one was looking and headed to Toronto alone. I didn't feel like having "that" conversation again.

As I drove my father's Pontiac Grand Am to the venue, I wondered if the gig would be worth the plunge into a new level of fandom. While I may be a massive fan, I'm not oblivious to the fact that most others in society view my actions with furrowed brows and question my sanity behind my back. Fiddling with the radio while switching Hip bootlegs, I heard a news tidbit on 102.1 The Edge:

"Rumour has it that tonight's Tragically Hip show at the ACC is being filmed for a live DVD. Stay tuned..."

Immediately, going alone to this gig had become worth it. *That Night in Toronto*, as the DVD would be titled, is a distinguished high point in the band's career. The gig itself was a greatest hits set; though I didn't hear a single new track that night, not being there would have haunted me forever. *That Night in Toronto* finally made its way into my hands almost ten months later while I was living in Poland. I sat alone, thousands of kilometres away from the ACC, and watched the concert in its entirety. I couldn't share the moment with anyone, but it didn't matter; not everything can be shared. The comfort and validation the DVD brought me was mine and mine alone.

The night after the Toronto gig, I drove to London from Guelph with Al, a friend from university with whom a meaningful relationship was beginning to form. It was his first Hip show. During the two-hour drive, we got to know each other better than we had in the previous two-and-a-half years. After meeting up with Johanna Wagstaffe for the requisite pre-show beers and burgers, the two Hip rookies asked me when my last Hip gig was. I told them I'd been to a gig alone the night before. Their jaws dropped. Perhaps they felt cheated on.

Still, I was able to tell them that if I hadn't gone, I wouldn't have been able to live with myself. For the first time, I admitted that going to Hip gigs wasn't something I liked to do, but was something I *had* to do. What's more, I said I didn't think I was going to stop anytime soon.

The two of them couldn't understand. And how could they? For the first time, it became clear how even those close to me viewed my obsession. They couldn't understand it, and therefore couldn't understand me. On the long, quiet, hungover drive back to Guelph, I wondered if I could always lean on this band, even from four rows away, or if soon I would have to give in and lean on people four inches away.

◆◆◆

Al wasn't the first person I'd bonded with over The Hip. On my second day in Poland, I met the other new teachers and we spent the entire day becoming familiar with one of Poland's better exports, its frothy lager.

I took an immediate liking to Richard, soft-spoken and crafty, from Liverpool. He had a warmth about him. His casual grace not only put me at ease, but made for some of the best conversations I've ever had. Plus, he was a dead ringer for Charlie Watts.

Our relationship took a gigantic leap with our first conversation. We talked music and both confessed a soft spot for early '90s rock, even agreeing that 1994 was the best year in recent memory for rock and roll. Being well into the day's drinking, I wasn't exercising much caution. "Oh yeah," I said. "'94 was when my band released their classic record."

Had I said this to friends in Canada, nobody would have blinked. But Rich's eyes widened.

"Your band? You were in a band in 1994?"

On the flight to Poland, I had wondered how long it would take before I was outed as a Hip fan; three pints, as it turned out.

"Well, no," I said. "My band, I mean, a band that I love and follow around on tour. The Tragically Hip. They released *Day for Night* in 1994."

"Oh, okay. The Tragically Hip. They're rather big in Canada, aren't they? I own one of their records, *Road Apples*. I picked it up at Amoeba Records in San Francisco. I'm quite fond of it."

What followed was a friendship that was both casual and weighty. Rich let me into his world and taught me about the person I wanted to become. On my last night in Poland before I left to follow The Hip on tour, we were into the pints again. I knew I'd have a hard time leaving Rich. I wanted him to remember me as a good friend, and as a Hip fan, since the band had sparked our friendship.

He asked me which track I'd love to hear on the tour. I'd been clamouring for "Three Pistols," the standout track from *Road Apples*.

"Three Pistols," I told him. "Definitely. I can't help but lose my shit for that track."

"Oh yeah. Which record is that one from?" he responded, without a trace of sarcasm.

I chuckled. I could not help how Rich would remember me. Though I remember him fondly, it's what he didn't remember that has stuck with me.

◆◆◆

Being obsessed with something can be dangerous. Expressing love and admiration can be charming, to an extent, but reveal too much and you risk social alienation.

People are quick to throw out the word "obsessed" and the negative connotations that follow it. Defending your obsession is futile, and only alienates you more; the harder you fight to defend yourself, the more bonkers people believe you are. It's a double-edged sword that you can't fight with.

This is why people are often guarded when divulging the intensity of their obsession in public. Sometimes, though, your desire to be seen as a functional member of society is overshadowed by strange and indefinable urges.

In the summer of 2004, I was working evenings for one of only two franchises in Ontario licensed to sell beer, aptly titled The Beer Store. It took a while for me to settle in at the giant orange and white booze peddler's. I was constantly distracted by a squirrely, unattainable girl two years my senior that would flirt, pull away, then always leave fifteen minutes early. I tried to keep a low profile and not reveal too much personal information, as love was on the line.

I was also working a mentally and physically draining job by day. Both jobs called for uniforms; I'd get one night a week where I could throw on one of my favourite t-shirts and sit on my roof with a beer and truly enjoy the summer I wanted to have as a twenty-year-old.

It was the first summer I'd lived away from home. I felt disconnected from my youth by this point, especially from my old Hip shirts. I had quite the collection, from a faded grey "*Music at Work*" tour shirt, a beige "1997 Another Roadside Attraction" tee, to a navy blue "*Day for Night*" shirt that was my first-ever online purchase. I wore that shirt to death, until one camping trip, when it disappeared. I mourned the loss of that piece of clothing as some might have mourned the loss of a childhood pet (had I been preoccupied with dogs like a normal boy, instead of a band and their clothing accessories).

I was lonely that summer. I'd usually collapse from exhaustion at the end of each day. Contrary to how I believed I would spend my first summer away from home, there were no barbecues with Hip albums spinning at full blast. By June, I was only listening to The Hip on my headphones in the morning. Knowing that this would be the only Hip I'd get for the day was more depressing than enlightening.

It was a typical evening in The Beer Store, making inane small talk with customers I knew I'd see again the next day. Bland familiarity had set in. I grabbed the six cans of cheap lager that another regular brought forward. It was all I could do to lift my head.

"How's it goin' man?" he asked. "You look a little rough."

Never before had any customer at the store talked about anything but themselves. I looked up. There he was: a plump, goofy looking fellow with a mess of grey hair and a bucktoothed smile. And there it was, wrapped tightly around his bulging belt: a navy blue "*Day for Night*" t-shirt.

A wave of spontaneity that I hadn't felt in months came over me. The girl I pined over stood behind me, polishing her nails, unaware of what was transpiring. I quickly envisioned myself leaping over the counter, beating the old dude for all he was worth and stealing the shirt in the process. It wasn't just a shirt. It was a way of life that I had lost and that he wore on his sweaty back. I needed The Hip; I needed the comfort they'd brought me. No one around me knew how I felt. I was alone in my search for a good summer; I was alone in my love for the band. I stopped the transaction and a line began to form.

"How much for that shirt?" I asked him.

"What?" he laughed, toying with my desperation. "This old shirt? Ha! I don't know. A million dollars!"

Everyone in line shared a laugh. If I'd had a blank cheque, a million dollars was what I would have written on the line.

"I'll give you twenty dollars for that shirt, right now."

Working two jobs is a mighty drag, but a thick wallet is one of the upsides.

"You're crazy, man."

I wasn't going to sell him his beer until this battle was finished. This was a matter of life and death. "I'll give you thirty dollars for that shirt."

"Are you serious?"

My legs grew stiff with resolve. If I were to salvage this summer, it would be with that shirt on my back. "I will give you forty bucks for that shirt."

By now, the entire store was quiet. My squirrely love stopped refining her nails and watched as her normally quiet and reserved co-worker was shedding his skin and letting his love of a band shine through.

The dude's mouth hung open, wondering whether to grab a quick forty bucks and walk home topless, or walk away and spread rumours of how bonkers that new guy at The Beer Store was.

"Come on man, give me my beer. It's just a shirt," he said timidly.

"I will give you fifty dollars for that shirt."

The whole store was intrigued as they realized how serious I was. Everyone traded excited glances. The battle now had a crowd. Who would blink first? The girl approached the standoff. I paid her no attention. I repeated myself: "I will give you FIFTY DOLLARS for that shirt."

Maybe he realized that he wouldn't get his lousy six-pack if he didn't give me the shirt. Or maybe he realized that my sanity was at a breaking point. For the last time, I made the offer: "I… will give YOU… FIFTY DOLLARS for that shirt."

"You're crazy, man!"

I didn't blink. I could feel him caving. I could feel my lonely self growing warmer with anticipation.

"Fuck man, you're crazy. You're nuts."

Yes, I told myself, *I am nuts*. But I was winning.

He stepped back and quickly lifted the shirt over his head before he could convince himself that, in the short term, walking home without a shirt was probably a little crazier.

He tossed it at me. I handed him the cash. He laughed again and kept repeating "that guy is crazy" as he left the store, his mammoth gut exposed and ripe for all the world to see. The thing is, I had never felt more sane.

The entire store exhaled. No one in line asked about the shirt. Instead, they all fixed their caps tight to their heads and got the hell out of there as quick as they could. And I put the girl far out of my mind.

I left fifteen minutes early that shift and biked home like a man possessed. The shirt was two sizes too large. I would end up seeing two Hip gigs that summer and two more that September. I grew into that t-shirt and vowed never to lose the shirt or that feeling ever again.

"[The Tragically Hip] played in Halifax. They were the band that came to town. We were up in rural Nova Scotia and nobody comes to town. Especially in the 90s, very rarely did a big band come through. But The Hip came through, every record. They made a point of coming out and playing the Metro Centre in Halifax. We waited by the phone until tickets went on sale and tried to buy tickets immediately. We'd make a family road trip, drive the two hours to Halifax from Antigonish for the show. We did that for two album cycles. By the second one, we got word from somebody where The Hip would be hanging out afterwards. They were hanging out at a place called The Press Gang in Halifax which is run by our bass player's dad so we had the inside scoop. So we go there to hang out and sure enough they all came in one at a time. Our minds were blown because this was the band that had just rocked the arena in town. That was my first time meeting The Hip. I was a fan, waiting around at the right place to shake their hands. And even back then I remember asking them, 'What does it sound like on the stage?' I'd only ever played in crappy clubs and my parents' basement. And they would tell us how it was kind of annoying and a bit echoey. Which was stuff I would discover is totally true."

— John-Angus MacDonald, The Trews

CHAPTER 6

Meet the Band

A strange thing happens to music with age. Young fans accept their band's word as gospel, because the myth surrounding them is too big for the members to be thought of as real people. However, as they get older, fans treat the band as they are: people with a job. Fans realize the barrier between the crowd and the stage is simply metaphorical. And because they've experienced some life-changing moments with the band in the background, it's time they debunk the myth and meet the band.

Some fans are lucky to be young when they meet their idols, while this barrier is still symbolic. Usually these meetings are pre-arranged; perhaps you win a radio contest (how accustomed I got to hearing busy signals when dialling up radio stations) or maybe a friend of a friend of someone whose mother once had coffee with the band *might* be able to get you a backstage pass.

In the beginning, meeting The Hip never seemed possible. Their music was big, their celebrity in suburban Southern Ontario even bigger. But by the time I was twenty-one, I had realized that The Hip were just five guys from Kingston, a city that could be reached from my hometown in about three hours. They didn't seem so intimidating; I was the guy who bought the tickets, knew the lyrics, wore the t-shirts. The Hip wouldn't be where they were if not for fans like me! I deserved to meet them, or so my naïve, entitled young self began to think.

◆◆◆

The Hip had booked a Canada Day gig in 2004, just two days after the release of *In Between Evolution*. Only twice in their history had the band played in Canada on Canada Day. Fuelling that kind of fervent patriotism never seemed high on the band's list of things to do, especially after the nastiness that had occurred a decade earlier.

The band was closing a large, all-day outdoor festival. As a drunk and rowdy crowd grew impatient with an eclectic line-up of musicians, legendary producer Daniel Lanois was booed and pelted with all manner of objects as he worked his way through his set. Gord Downie dedicated The Hip's first song to "the asshole that throws shit at musicians." It's understandable that the band would be hesitant to play such a gig again.

It had been almost ten months since I'd seen the band live. And with a new record out, it was going to be a Hip-intensive few months. This is the best time of an obsessed fan's life. What's more, I was at a point where I was ready to embrace something new.

Just a few weeks before the release of *In Between Evolution*, I had broken up with a girlfriend. It was the first time I'd ever done the "breaking." Normally relationships of mine had a way of working themselves out, usually because of my own incapacity to consider anyone else's feelings. Still, I felt like a winner. I didn't want a girlfriend for the first time since I'd ever wanted girls. *In Between Evolution*? I understood that.

Days before the concert, my ex-girlfriend let me know that not only was she coming to the Canada Day gig, but through a friend, she'd scored backstage passes as well. The dagger was sharp and laden with rust; it easily found its way into my heart.

I went on the attack, saying awful, hurtful things:

"Why are you doing this to me? Are you trying to make me jealous?"

"You know I deserve that backstage pass, and if you don't take me, there's no chance I'll ever talk to you again."

"You don't even like The Hip like I do."

I went from winner of the break-up to a whiny, desperate parody of a man. Gone was all of the joyous anticipation that usually surrounds the days leading up to a Hip concert.

On Canada Day, driving into Toronto, I still didn't know if she'd give me one of her two backstage passes. I felt no patriotism, just insurmountable nerves. In my mind, not meeting the band backstage could only have two outcomes:

1. Blowing my first shot at meeting the band and not having another opportunity to meet them for a long time, if ever.
2. Having no one to blame but myself.

Still, I'd brought a camera and my *Day for Night* liner notes, holding out hope that I'd be granted my chance.

The show had been a banger, but I couldn't focus on anything but what *might* happen. After the gig, my party met up with hers. Between us stood her "friend," that cagey, shifty character with the lowest of moral standards. We all know "the friend." The one who's always luckier, but never really deserves to be. But he held the key to the Promised Land.

We all stared at one another. I had to do something to make my case for that extra backstage pass. Still too proud to beg, I lamented that I'd never met the band and all I wanted to do was thank them for the countless memories they'd given me. My friends looked empathetic, though there was a look in their eyes that suggested I could do more. So, for the first time in months (including the time when we were still together), I smiled at my ex-girlfriend. Yes, I was cringing behind it. But then she smiled. And the "friend" took notice.

He took a dramatic step back and announced with unnecessary grandeur for all the drunks stumbling out of the venue to hear, "I tell you what, man. She says you're a good guy, and you're a big fan. So I'm gonna do this for you. You're goin' to see The Hip backstage!"

Backstage pass stickered to my shoulder, my ex and I walked through the empty seats. We didn't say much. I should have talked about the gig. I should have talked about us. But I remained silent.

I was a fraud and anything that came out of my mouth would have just been more of a lie. I was on my way to meet my heroes for the first time, though by that point I didn't feel like the fan I had been for the past eleven years. As we flashed our passes for the bouncer and crossed the threshold into a swarm of industry types, good-looking chatty types and finally, wide-eyed first-timers, I had no idea who I really was.

My ex-girlfriend relinquished authority and waited on my every move. Behind Ricky Wellington, The Hip's massive security guard, and a narrow door, there appeared to be a more exclusive area. The slick and suited-up disappeared through that door, as did the families with young children. After twenty minutes of waiting in line, the last silver-lined backstage-pass holders disappeared, and only the wide-eyed ones, clutching purple passes, were left. I realized I was part of a pre-arranged meet and greet.

Still, Gord Downie appeared through the narrow doorway. I clutched the *Day for Night* liner notes tightly. He stood there, looking as exhausted as one might be after a physically draining two-hour set. He was clad in the Canadian tuxedo of jeans and jean jacket. I readied myself for my five minutes with my Mick Jagger, my Michael Jordan, my Winston Churchill, my hero.

"Hi Gord."

Good opener.

"Hi, what's your name?"

"I'm Joshua."

"Hi Jason."

"No, it's Joshua."

"Sorry. Joshua."

There was the hiccup. My time was limited. It looked as if I would only have one real question for him. I glanced at my sweaty palms, clutching the *Day for Night* booklet. It came to me: *In Between Evolution* was the first Hip record with a "Parental Advisory" warning on the front, due to Gord's use of expletives throughout the record. I had my question, though in retrospect I can't believe I didn't have a thousand others waiting in the bullpen.

"So I noticed you did a lot of cursing on the new record. How did you explain that to your kids?"

"I told my kids that swearing is only valid when it's absolutely necessary."

"Funny you should say that..."

Day for Night was a Christmas gift from my parents in 1994. Though my normally reserved folks had decided to shove me into the world of rock and roll, it came at a price. As soon as I opened the album, it was snatched away from me. Censorship was a mighty tool of oppression during my formative years; my parents went to work on the liner notes, running a black marker through anything resembling an expletive. In my house, swearing was as bad as it got. And as poetic as the tunes were, my folks just couldn't rationalize

Gord's logic. Some of the glaring omissions included:

"Brutal as depicted truth, that kid's a [redacted] goof!"

"There's a trace o' mint wafting in from the North so we don't [redacted] with the 401"

Or the one that really got me:

"There's this [redacted] band you gotta see, they used to scare the living [redacted] outta me!"

I wanted desperately to reach Gord on a personal level. I told him how important the album had been to me growing up. I thanked him for all that he and his band had done, and told him how I had considered giving my father a copy of *In Between Evolution* with the expletives markered out, maybe as a means to foster his own discovery, or maybe just to spite him. Gord chuckled as I wrapped up my story.

"Well, you've got a good father there."

He autographed the booklet, signing it "Josh for night."

Gord looked relaxed and we spoke a little longer about the new record. I was curious about "Fighter, Fighter," a B-side from the record that fans hadn't heard yet, but was still generating buzz. Apparently one of the band's harder and more daring tracks, Gord went on to tell me that the song told the story of a small girl during the Rwandan Genocide many years earlier.

"*Qu'est-ce-que tu vas faire*? (What are you gonna do?)" went the chorus, Gord told me. He spoke with a quiet thoughtfulness. "I really don't know why that one got left off the record," he said, looking down. His fondness for the track was strong enough to send him into a makeshift air-guitar solo on the spot, singing pieces. Our conversation shed light on a fact that many already knew. Being Gord Downie was not a day job, it was a way of life. Here was an artist comfortable enough with his celebrity to always be his eccentric, invigorating self no matter the occasion. I stood in awe.

Sure, he had mistaken my name, but I could die tomorrow and still get access to Hip heaven because Downie had played "Fighter, Fighter" on air guitar for me, and no other fan (or so I hoped). This was the "Gord moment" I'd hoped for, and all it took for me to realize that good things do happen backstage. But there was no sense in pushing my luck. I shook his hand and moved on. I was dazed; my feet moved without guidance. Everything I'd ever wanted as a young dude now seemed possible. Everything that is, except documentation. I'd forgotten a photograph.

I interrupted a conversation Gord was having with another eager fan.

"I'm sorry, Gord," I said. "But I didn't get a photo. Could you spare a second?"

"Sure thing, Jason."

This time, I didn't have the heart to correct him. But Gord wasn't to blame; the entire situation was marked with a giant asterisk. I'd meet the rest of my friends later and regale them with the story of "Fighter, Fighter," but I knew it was all a sham.

Because I treated the opportunity to meet a member of the band in a shallow manner I left feeling grateful, but not fulfilled. This was not a display of me as a fan. I had tried my damndest to be honest with Gord but I was not being honest with myself.

The next and last time I saw the girl, I was too drunk to stand, let alone have a conversation. The next time I tried to talk to Gord after a show, he stormed through a group of fans, eager to get to the tour bus and jet back home to Canada. Karma made a mockery of me, as I'd made a mockery of my ex-girlfriend. You could argue that there's no correlation, but if I'm truthful I insist that there must be.

◆◆◆

One of the biggest problems with the "meet and greet" is that they're one-sided affairs. Fans, full of expectations, are ready to shower their gods with praise. And those very gods are usually contractually obliged to attend. Not an ideal two-way relationship.

Rock and roll gods are usually bombarded with swarms of fans in a short amount of time, quickly reducing those fans to mere numbers. To bands, obsessed fans are just part of the job.

Coming to this realization hurts. It can distance fans from the band. Cynical thoughts run through their heads:

"I could have been replaced at any gig I've ever attended."

"The band only thanks their fans because we keep them in business."

"I don't buy a concert ticket, I pay their salaries."

Although I came to terms with the fact that, at an early age, The Hip meant more to me than everything else in my life, I also came to terms with the fact that while the band appreciated their fans, personally, I didn't bear nearly the same importance as they did to me.

On the afternoon of the Air Canada Centre '04 show, I waited at the Edge, a Toronto radio station located a fifteen minute walk from the venue. Word got out that The Hip would be appearing in the studio for a quick chat, but it seemed word had not travelled far. Even though there were only a handful of us waiting around, I wondered: was I part of another contractual obligation? Or could this be one of those spontaneous meetings for which The Hip had long been renowned in obsessed circles: one where they converse with fans like people, instead of faces in the crowd?

There was a calm, nonchalant feeling in the station. It was a stark contrast to the last time I'd visited the Edge studios for an artist interview.

My sister had been obsessed with Blink 182 as a kid.

Though I can't fault her now, it was hard for me to support her. When the band farted on stage, I always thought *that* was the best part of the show. But I enabled her addiction, going to gigs with her and attending radio interviews. We waited in the crowded studio for well over an hour before the band showed up. They were greeted by mass hysteria. A sense of pandemonium swept the tiny studios. My sister didn't even try to fight back tears as Mark Hoppus brushed against her right shoulder.

Although my sister knew every word to every song, created collages of cut-out photos of the band and insisted there were songs within Blink 182's repertoire that were written with her in mind, to the band she was just another high-pitched scream. Her connection to the band was intense and personal, but it was not reciprocated. The band itself was so popular that, unfortunately for her, the connection lost steam because everyone around her was experiencing those same emotions and expressing them in the same way. It hurt me to watch her fall for this band and then watch her admiration become displaced not long afterwards. It was as if the louder she screamed, the farther the band moved away from her.

Gord Sinclair and Rob Baker emerged from a black sedan ten minutes before the interview started. No applause greeted them. A few fans asked for autographs or photos, which they both obliged. I watched in amazement; it felt more like two-fifths of Canada's biggest band were entering their local pub for an afternoon drink.

Although they did dozens of radio interviews for this tour (I heard both Rob and Gord on the radio in London the next night), they treated this part of the job with honest enthusiasm. Then it dawned on me: they had to be there, but the handful of us waiting to get a word in did not. And they respected that. We stood in Toronto, where The Hip draw their biggest crowds. We were in the most popular radio station in the city. We, who numbered no more than ten. If only ten people would show up on their most popular turf, how few would there be on some of their smaller touring stops? We crowded around them while they did the interview. It felt warm, friendly.

After the short interview, there was no testy road manager waiting to shuffle the band to their next appointment. The band stepped away from the DJ and waited for a fan to pounce. For a moment, nobody did anything. The rock stars were ready and the fans were either too overwhelmed by possibilities or too polite to want to ruin someone else's opportunity. I had to act fast, lest my questions blend into another fan's. I thought about waiting for Gord Downie a few months earlier. I needed some confidence to ensure things wouldn't end up as they had last time. I took a step to the right, and Gord Sinclair was there.

We shook hands. "Hi Gord, I'm Joshua."

"Hey Joshua, how are ya?"

I entered the alternate universe that exists only when you meet someone you look up to. You function well, and manage to carry on a conversation. And though you have a faint idea of when the conversation has gone on for "too long," time has ceased to exist. I imagine it's similar to the zone a good pitcher gets into, where he can see nothing but the batter and hear nothing but the satisfying clamp of his catcher's glove or the disappointing crack of a bat.

Gord and I talked about the tour and how the band's crowds had changed over the years. He set the tone when he said, "I find now that more and more of the fans in the crowd these days actually *listen* to our tunes."

And as I spoke, something remarkable happened: Gord *listened* to my questions. And when he answered, he looked in my eyes. Sure, he didn't ask me any questions. But the look on his face said I was not just a fan, but a person with thoughts about his band that he was open to hearing. This conversation felt more meaningful than ninety-three percent of the conversations I'd ever had.

The important thing about the alternate universe is not to break the spell. Your nerves must be kept close to you, but it was all I could do not to stop him mid-sentence and yell out of the studio onto Yonge Street: "It's fucking Gord Sinclair! Holy fucking shit!"

The truth became apparent during that relaxed conversation: treat celebrities as celebrities, and they will treat you as fans. Mark Hoppus and Tom DeLonge did not answer a single question from any of the screaming girls in that radio studio, because no questions were asked. The only sound audible was that of delirium. It's hard to take someone seriously in that regard. But treat bands as people, and they will generally do the same. So I did what people do. I asked him for a favour.

"I'm sure you have tonight's set worked out, but I'm going to tomorrow's gig in London. I've got a request. I've never heard 'Daredevil' live. Think you could play it?"

Now, I did go for the jugular here. Gord Sinclair not only writes the setlists, but his thick bass work is omnipresent throughout the rumbling drive of "Daredevil."

"Yeah, okay. We played it the other night in Winnipeg and it went pretty well. I'll see what we can do."

With that, I thanked him and moved on. Now seemingly a pro at chatting with my heroes, my conversation with Rob was even longer and more relaxed.

These simple exchanges briefly allowed me into their world. I had been so nervous driving to the studio, waiting for them to arrive and listening to them speak to the DJ. But after speaking to the band, I felt more like a person than a fan.

Maybe the band would play "Daredevil" the next night, and maybe they wouldn't. Still, to know that they had played to millions of fans for over twenty years but could still take the time to approach those fans as individuals, gave me a newfound respect for them. Did my sister respect Blink 182 when they did a similar interview in the same studio? Hard to say, but the number of fart jokes they made on air leads me to believe otherwise. Fans get so wrapped up in adoring everything that we forget respect bridges the gap between fans and heroes.

I left the studio. I needed to walk and let my intense fanhood breathe after forcefully subduing it for fifteen minutes. I was two steps from the door, ready to hit Yonge Street, when I heard someone behind me shout.

"Hey, Josh!"

I turned back. Gord Sinclair was smiling at me.

"Good request."

The next night, the band came onstage for a second encore and began the slow intro to "Daredevil." Gord Sinclair hadn't just listened, he had remembered. I began shaking my two friends incessantly. And being only four rows from the stage, I shouted at the top of my lungs, over the building intro: "Thank you, Gord Sinclair! Thank you!"

He looked up from his bass, smiled, and nodded. There are times to play it cool, and there are times to let loose. I'd barely spoken above a whisper in that studio a day earlier. Now I had to shout and remind myself that at heart, I was a fan. And when "Daredevil" happened, I was reminded that being a fan is something worth screaming about.

◆◆◆

I have yet to cover the most fervent and obsessive approach to meeting a band: waiting for them after the gig, behind the venue. Whereas pre-arranged meet-and-greets are usually appreciated by casual fans, waiting behind the venue draws skepticism and only occurs in the company of other obsessed fans, or their quiet girlfriends and boyfriends along for the ride. The first time I dragged my wife Jess to wait for a band, she was terribly reluctant. But I knew that if we didn't meet the band she would never be able to share the unique glimpses into their life that I cherished.

Yet, sometimes patient fans are left in the cold for hours, only to be told by the band's manager or bodyguard that they'd appreciate it if we, the obsessed, would get lost. Sometimes, bands leave their lives on the stage behind and a clear path to the tour bus is all they desire.

The Hip have always enjoyed a healthy relationship with their fans. I've never heard of admirers behind the venue being treated like garbage. Fans that wait outside after the gig are usually after real answers to real questions. They are unsatisfied with radio interviews and with just seeing the band onstage. They demand personification of the relationship they've created with the band's music. After all, they likely formed a personal relationship the moment they first heard the band.

After my first overseas gig in London, England, in July 2006, I met three members of the band. I waited with a few other devoted fans to meet Gord Sinclair. I thanked him for playing "Daredevil" two years previous. He gave me a confused look and told me I'd just given him a "headtrip." Paul followed and after I caught a waft of some pot from behind the venue doors, we shared an awkward conversation. I reverted back to my teenage ways and told him that lighting his smoke would be an honour.

Finally, when Rob came out, I told him that I had loved the gig and that I had a few more gigs to see on the tour. He told me that they had "a million more to go" with some enthusiasm. Gord Downie emerged soon afterwards and was practically mauled.

It all felt rushed and impersonal, but nobody was to blame. The band had just begun a European tour and were probably as confused by their new surroundings as I was. Still, something inside me said "make this better." That night

I went back to my overpriced hostel and thought about the reasons why Hip fans would travel across the world to see a band they could probably see a few months later, maybe fifteen minutes from their home. I realized The Hip command such intense devotion from their fans that they must keep sharing the object of their devotion with other people.

Fourteen months later I was back in London, this time with Jess. Instead of being on our way home, we were stopping over in the city before another year abroad. While we could have left much later for our one-year teaching contracts in Istanbul, timing the beginning of this trip with The Hip's European tour was no coincidence.

After another stellar performance from the band, we waited behind the venue. Sweaty and jet-lagged from the awful red-eye flight across the Atlantic, a strange, ominous feeling washed over me. I smoked too many cigarettes and waited.

That trip to London was a microcosm of my life as a whole. Now twenty-three and a university graduate, I left family and friends in Ontario to travel with a woman who seemed ready to share the rest of her life with me. I knew my days of waiting for The Hip behind the venue and dropping hundreds of dollars on gigs were numbered. Even though they were in the midst of a full European tour, this was the only show I would be taking in. I would spend a year abroad, and the thought of returning to Southern Ontario made my stomach turn. Sure, it was The Hip's default touring homebase, but there were greater forces at work. Jess was waiting patiently in the drizzle of an autumn London evening for this band; for the first time, I began to think of someone besides myself and of something besides The Hip.

Our small talk consisted mostly of my stories of The Hip's past. She listened, but I knew she was thinking about the daring new city we would call home in a few days. I spoke about the band with reverence, but every story now seemed distant. I would later realize that sharing those stories in the drizzle was an exercise in coming to terms with a reality I feared would happen eventually: I would see The Hip less and less. They would continue to be an important part of my life, but The Hip were always *my* dream, *my* band. With another person to consider, I knew that shared joys would emerge and this might be the last time I'd wait for the band. It was fitting then, that we were the only people waiting that night.

My mission became clear: I had to introduce Jess to the band. Fans wait behind the venue to share their happiness and to let the band know how important that happiness is. She needed to see The Hip as people, not celebrities. By introducing her, I would reveal in greater detail the personal relationship I'd formed with the band's music. I'd finally met someone who was as important to me as The Hip were. It would be my final, hopelessly romantic gesture: one last attempt to show this woman (and in effect, anyone else I'd ever been close to) how much The Hip meant to me.

As members of the crew began to emerge from the venue, we readied ourselves for the band. Jess bit her nails.

"Are you nervous?" I asked.

"No!" she shot back, with a look that told me to drop the issue.

Paul came out first. He lit a cigarette and stood alone.

I approached him, lit a smoke of my own and introduced Jess. We began a light-hearted conversation. I asked the question that'd been on my mind: which member of the band had the biggest record collection?

What followed were stories about The Hip's studio, The Bathhouse, outside of Kingston, where Rob housed most of his records. Jess stood listening quietly behind me.

When fans wait eagerly for bands after the show, the nature of the relationship is that the band is the fan's superior. In town for just one night, the band will be surrounded by different fans in a different city the following night. The band has all the answers; they are the ones with everything to offer.

But as Paul and I smoked, we started to talk about things other than music.

"Tonight was great, Paul. And I'm happy it was. This might be our last Hip gig for a while," I admitted.

He looked confused, until we told him we were moving to Istanbul. Paul was interested in what had brought us to London and what was taking us to Istanbul. With a new sense of familiarity we each lit up another cigarette.

Seconds later, the venue's back door swung open, backing Paul into a corner. A smiling Gord Sinclair emerged. He saw Paul behind the door, cigarette dangling from his mouth with no room to move.

"Oh, sorry Paul," he offered.

"It's okay. I feel a little like a bass player here."

We all laughed. Though I'd met the band before, I had never seen them interact. It was all so loose and comfortable. They shared swift exchanges as only band mates of twenty-plus years could.

I introduced myself to Gord Sinclair (again, but such is the reality of being a fan—you remember them, but it's unlikely they remember you) and Paul spoke up, "They're on their way to Istanbul."

"No way. So cool," said Gord.

"Yeah," I said. "You guys ever thought of playing there? I know there'd be at least two people in attendance."

"I dunno," said Gord with a grin. "What do you think, Paul? It would take a lot of work, right?"

They both snickered. From my end, it was as if Gord was the captain of the flight and Paul was the loveable stoner who only did as much work as was required. It all made sense. My girl and I saw band dynamics like never before.

Soon, Gord and Paul's wives emerged and introductions were made. The conversation turned back to Istanbul. When we had left for London we were terribly unsure about whether going to Istanbul was the right move. But as the women talked about the exotic markets Istanbul was sure to offer, and Paul, Gord and I moved back and forth between jokes and music chit-chat, I felt a newfound sense of confidence about our move. The band that had provided me with so much inspiration over the years seemed interested in my life.

By the end of our conversation, they asked *me* if I wanted a photo. We shook hands and said our goodbyes. Although I'd had a hard time leaving my friends and family in Canada, this was one goodbye that really stung.

"There's a professionalism [The Tragically Hip] bring to the table. But even with all of that there's something very intimate as well. Maybe it's specifically something with Gord that he brings but all of their performances are very 'in the moment.' He finds something special with the night. That's what a great show is. You've seen bands phone it in but they always felt very connected. They have something that's beyond their songs and albums. What they're doing with their fans is very raw."

— Paul Murphy, Wintersleep

CHAPTER 7

Make Your Way to the Front

Great concerts can change the world, but they're often terribly impersonal. Great Hip gigs have not changed the world in a broad sense, but they have changed the lives of many people who have attended.

I wasn't at Woodstock. I wasn't at Altamont. I wasn't at the Newport Folk Festival. I'd love to talk to people who were, though. I'd ask them how the *concert* was. Not about the ramifications afterwards or how the world was a better or worse place because of the event. I'd ask them about the performances and relay The Hip's ethos that a concert is one night and one night only. A random group of strangers tied together in the belief that something magical can happen. As great as it can be, the evening only lasts so long. Memories of a great night of live music carry more weight than any write-up in any history book. Live music is personal in nature. Any time the myth of a gig grows larger than the gig itself, the memories become obsolete.

You could argue that with the wealth of music and the number of concerts available to fans, it's becoming tougher for a concert to change the world. Live music as an art form hasn't lost any of its social importance, but it's definitely not gaining any steam.

So why do concerts matter anymore? And why do they matter so much to me, enough to forgo social obligations, spend thousands of dollars, and throw my sanity by the wayside, all for the sake of getting through those doors to watch a band play music? I've met great, upstanding citizens who've never been to a concert. But they've seen movies, read books, and probably even bought an album on iTunes. Why haven't they succumbed to the lure of the gig?

Perhaps they were never drawn to spend money on a concert ticket, which begets transportation to the gig, which often requires the pre-gig meal, and which, in my case, always results in buying a t-shirt. Standing in a crowd of people you've never met, listening to a band you could listen to in the comfort of your own home, can be an acquired taste.

I will be the first to admit that standing in those crowds is a risk. After all, I have had some bad experiences. But I chose to give myself over to the time inside the venue, where fans roll the dice and hope for a slice of transcendence. It doesn't always happen, but the least fans can do is hope that the memories of the night will last longer than the ringing in their ears.

My appreciation for gigs has even spawned a career. Writing for music publications has meant that going to gigs and spending nights in bars, clubs, and arenas has become a way of life. It always feels surreal to get paid to review concerts. After all, a memory is intangible and cannot be bought or sold. And for a band like The Hip, which has built its career on the power and passion of its live sets, the memories built around gigs sustain and reward their fans.

These are not The Hip's "best" gigs. What follow are the gigs that rendered me helpless. Thousands of kilometres away, it is likely that other music fans were experiencing gigs that produced a similar effect. But for these gigs, there was nowhere else in the world I would have rather been.

The Last Gig of the Music at Work Tour
Air Canada Centre
Toronto, Ontario
December 23rd, 2000

My first two Hip gigs were eye opening experiences. I had been exposed to the world of Hip fans, albeit from the cheap seats. To a seventeen-year-old who was attracted to bands that played arenas instead of clubs, those two nights were journeys into the great unknown.

It was once very easy to get excited about arena gigs, though the buzz inside is not organic; from the moment the doors open, the smell of stale arena food and frothy beer fills the air. Inside an arena normally reserved for competition, everyone in a concert crowd is a winner simply for buying a ticket. The hum of pre-set expectations from new fans and the calming confidence of the old-timers sets these grand old barns on fire. Rock and roll fans rent the room for one night and try to cull every victory granted to its usual inhabitants, hoping that this will lead to a night they'll never forget. Arena gigs are big, but only because they have to be: the expectations are just that large.

At those two arena shows, I roared along to the hits, stood at attention in the encore breaks and agonized over what they might play when they reappeared. After studying dozens of setlists, I began to have an idea. Not just about encore tunes, but about how to best take in a show of this magnitude.

Now, I couldn't really *see* the band during those first two gigs. Given the depth of my passion, I tried not to look at the large video screens side-stage. Somehow, squinting seemed more in line with the experience I thought fans like me should be having.

On December 23rd, perhaps because I'd gotten my tickets the day before, I was granted my first good seats to a gig:

twelfth row, stage left. As me and Payne-O, my bassist friend of three years, were shown down the aisle towards our seats, I felt every tiny hair on my tiny teenage frame rise to attention. We weren't just close to the action, we were creating our own vibe.

Music at Work was an expansive, eclectic record. The band replicated that sound onstage during the tour. They brought keyboardist Chris Brown and vocalist Kate Fenner to accompany them throughout their set. They dove deep into their back catalogue and didn't look back. What's more, The Hip had no opening act for these gigs.

For years, opening for The Hip has been one of the biggest Catch 22's in Canadian rock and roll. From the moment they come onstage, people subject the opening act to a demoralizing and horribly uninventive chant:

"HIP! HIP! HIP!"

I'll admit it can be a rousing call to arms. But to disrespect opening bands with a "HIP!" chant during their set is an offense to the years they've spent getting to that stage. I have seen opening bands booed off the stage before The Hip have appeared, and I have seen the audience applaud much too loudly when the openers have told the crowd, "This is our last song." (As happened to the wonderful Julie Doiron during my first Hip gig.)

Perhaps sensing that their fame was going south, the band had decided that this tour was going to be all about them. With seven full-length studio records, they had more than enough material to work with. Fans who had been clamouring for rarely heard tracks were forming personal checklists. With the band playing over thirty songs a night on the tour, everything (even your favourite, grossly-underplayed songs) seemed possible. I chanted "HIP!" wildly along with everyone else.

In our seats Payne-O and I were gripped by the significance of the situation. Seated around us were no drunken louts. Young families and elderly people took their seats calmly, with a sense of pride and honour. I felt the same way, but as a seventeen-year-old fan, I wasn't nearly as dignified.

I ducked out for a pretzel. On the way back, I asked the usher if there was anything special about the section we were in.

"You're sitting in the same section as the members of The Hip's family," he said.

It was all I could do not to piss my pants before telling Payne-O. We were among the elite.

Graduating from the cheap seats to the "we're lucky we clicked the 'purchase' button on Ticketmaster at the exact moment we did" seats was a strange feeling. A sense of entitlement quickly swept over us, like teenagers who get into a bar or club illegally for the first time. But for all the pride we felt, we couldn't help but be nervous. What if we didn't act the part? Could they sniff out first-timers?

As the lights went down, I stared into a sea of possibility.

Even though it was only my third Hip gig, my level of anticipation and dedication (and knowledge of inane Hip trivia, like the fact that Gord drinks blue Gatorade after a gig and that Paul's favourite Rolling Stones album is *Exile on Main Street)* was right up there with some of the long-time Hipheads. I also knew how often the band had played "Three Pistols": only three times that tour and four long years before, during their last gig at the legendary Maple Leaf Gardens.

Where I had the old-timers beat was with my exuberance. I was young and didn't give a shit about keeping my composure. Back then, I'd leave the house with my Walkman, listening to bootlegs from the *Trouble at the Henhouse* tour and dancing as I walked. "Three Pistols" was one of those tracks with an intrinsic power over me. Rousing and compelling, rarely does the song not grab me by the balls. I fear the day I'm at a funeral and someone has it programmed as their ringtone. I can only hope I don't know the deceased that well.

I knew the band would take us on a ride that night, but was oblivious to where we were headed. Three songs in, Gord stepped up to the mic and began mumbling something about Quebec being "home to some of the world's finest beers," before telling the packed house: "'Trois Pistoles. This is 'Three Pistols,' ladies and gentlemen."

I nearly fell onto someone seated in front of me. In the second before Paul's intoxicating guitar intro, I let out a feverish "Yeaaahhh!" for the entire arena to hear. I've always wanted to bottle the emotion running through my veins that night, but it floated away like the pot smoke in the air. That is until I downloaded the bootleg a few months later. In the pause between Downie's opener and Paul's chugging riff to kick off the song, a voice is heard yelling at the top of his lungs. I am convinced that it is me, despite the razzing I get from friends whenever I play it. Maybe, just once, the smoke in the air clung to something permanent.

Locked inside the arena, I stayed in my spot for two-and-a half hours. No piss breaks, no cigarettes. That level of focus wasn't so demanding back then, but now I realize what a feat it was.

The set that night was a wave. They dipped deep into their back catalogue, playing five tracks I haven't heard live since. Through the barrage of new tunes, old favourites, and rarities that elated Hipheads, the band was testing the crowd's patience and appreciation.

That tour was a snapshot of a band at the height of their popularity. Sure, the *Trouble at the Henhouse* tour was longer, and their previous record, *Phantom Power*, had spawned more singles. But on that night, just hours before Christmas Day, the band gave fans exactly what they wanted: a marathon of music and a lifetime of memories.

Some nights I've watched in awe at how easy The Hip make timeless rock look. But what sets that night apart is how hard the band worked. So close to the holiday season, they were able to shrug off whatever concerns they might have had and leave their souls on the stage. From slow, chugging numbers like "Yawning or Snarling" to the intense second-set closer, "On the Verge," their approach knew no boundaries.

The fans replied in kind. Toronto fans have always claimed The Hip as their own, and the band has played into this enthusiasm. Every time they play "Bobcaygeon" anywhere near Toronto, fans lose their collective shit. Sure enough, as the twenty-sixth (!) song of the night, the crowd responded to "Bobcaygeon" with a deafening roar. Someone seated behind me decided that his overpriced beer wasn't worth drinking and chucked it into the crowd. I was mid-roar when the beer drenched my brand-new Hip hockey jersey, a gift from my then-girlfriend. (Gracious as she was, she presented me with a size medium, despite my puny adolescent frame.) Payne-O responded with a shocked, conciliatory look, but I just smiled. I thought about all the beers I'd be able to treat recklessly at future Hip gigs, when I actually reached drinking age. The line "that Night in Toronto" might have seemed like grandstanding, but it now had a place in my concert memory.

By getting closer to the action, I had learned just how *expansive* The Hip could be. Not just in sound, but in scope. I've seen many other bands more than three times, but it was that third gig that officially had me hooked. I was now attached on a personal level. I counted myself lucky, but I still wanted more. I was addicted, and if that gig taught me anything, it was that there was much more in which I could indulge.

My father picked us up afterwards and smelled the beer as soon as we got in the car. As goofy as his son was, he knew I wouldn't have spilled a beer down my own back. I slept in my jersey that night and refused to wash it, until my mother hijacked it for a load of whites months later. I never wanted the smell of that night to disappear. In a way, it never did.

Second Gig of the In Between Evolution Tour
The Odeon
Cleveland, Ohio
September 19th, 2004

The more intense a fan I became, the more intense a concert experience I demanded. By 2004, I was in the midst of an early-twenties identity crisis and The Hip were the only thing I could count on. While I felt like jettisoning every other part of my personality, I knew that I was going to be a Hip fan, no matter how much I needed to mature. In fact, my obsession was growing.

At arena gigs, you are guaranteed a seat. For the timid, this is important. But what you soon realize when walking into a small club for the first time is how much more control you have: where you'll sit or stand, whether you'll move around to get photos—even when you'll make trips to the bar or washroom. I waited outside the Odeon the afternoon of the show; I was determined, for the first time, to spend an entire concert in the front row.

It was an inevitable graduation. I needed to have nothing between me and the band. If there were no heads in front of me, then there would be nothing stopping this gig from becoming permanently etched in my memory.

When the doors to the Odeon opened, I nearly bowled over other fans in my fight to be up front. I stared at lifeless instruments; I conjured up fantastic images and sounds to accompany them. I looked around at other unblinking fans. Their eyes too were focused on what was before us.

It would be another two-and-a-half hours before The Hip would even grace the stage, but already this gig had become tangible. I caressed the barrier rail before me, though to onlookers it probably appeared as if I was hanging on for dear life.

During cramped gigs, everything is immediate. I couldn't close my eyes and mentally wander during a guitar solo or mull over every one of Gord's mid-song musings. Being upfront required a level of attentiveness that I was unaccustomed to. Around nine o'clock, the lights went down and the band came on.

The five members of The Hip stood before me like giants; grizzled men on a mission. I could clearly see who the band was and they would finally get a chance to see me the way I'd always wanted to appear: as an impassioned fan. With everything I could summon, I hollered as loud and grinned as wide as I could. Gord stepped to the mic.

"Hello," he said. "It can't be Nashville every night. I learned that, last night, in Detroit."

Gord had no idea of the hell I had gone through in Detroit the night before, but for a lead singer who constantly speaks in metaphors, it seemed like an appropriate start. I reminded myself to keep my footing with now-slick hands clutching the rail.

It took a few songs for the enormity of the evening to kick in. Not only was this the intimate American gig that I'd always dreamed of attending but the band was on fire, too. Sweat dripped onto the stage. This was a gig for the hardcore fans; deep cuts like "Vapour Trails" and "Looking for a Place to Happen" exemplified the band's ability to turn loose jams into razor-sharp live performances.

Midway through the set, Gord said they were going to play a new song, then launched into "Fighter, Fighter" for the first time as The Tragically Hip. (A year earlier, during a surprise two-night charity stand in Whistler, the band had played the song billed as The Fighter Fighters.)

A strange feeling came over me. Was "Fighter, Fighter" indeed happening? I didn't think about who I would brag to afterwards, as I had in the past, but instead became locked in the moment. My whole life as a Hip fan had been one long fight for these kinds of personal connections with the music. Now, I had connected the dots; I had a concert moment no one could ever take away from me.

While there is no way that the band could have known I'd be in attendance, "Fighter, Fighter" still found its way onto the setlist. I looked at the band, smiled (as I couldn't sing along) and realized that as one single person, changing the world is tough. But as one person, changing your own world is indeed possible. You've just got to get close enough to the action.

Paradiso
Amsterdam, Netherlands
July 11th, 2006

As I tried to navigate the winding streets of Amsterdam in the July heat, I felt a heaviness on my shoulders. I'd been drunk and stoned for a week. Exhausted and off-course, the heaviness was the weight of a year spent abroad and alone, trying to figure out what was important. In three days I'd be back home in Canada, surrounded by family with a barrage of never-ending questions.

Whatever I'd learned or hadn't would have to wait. I met the rest of a travelling troupe of Canadian Hip fans in front of the Paradiso. I must have looked like hell.

Paradiso, a converted church, is older than rock and roll itself. Gorgeous stained-glass windows line the walls behind the stage. Rustic white railings line the balcony and wafts of smoke paint the air. Friends I'd travelled with during the last week were beside me and rabid fans were above and behind me. My beer sat directly in front of me, leaning against a monitor on stage.

The band came on. What followed was ninety minutes of The Hip at their most sublime and flawless. Everything that could go right did. I had written my own movie over the past year and now I had a great ending.

The Tragically Hip, the band that had provided the soundtrack to my every struggle and hope while growing up, were just feet away from me. I smiled at the band. They smiled back. They were taking "Grace, too" to new heights, setting free a sound I'd only dreamed existed. I was thousands of kilometres away from home. It felt so complete. The show was everything that live music should be: timeless, in that the memory is strong, but still fleeting, because great live gigs cannot truly be captured.

I learned at Paradiso why fans exist: it is our duty to capture those fleeting moments. We were there when Gord disappeared so the band could own the stage through the extended jam of "The Last of the Unplucked Gems." We were there when they dedicated "Lionized" to "Zizou," (Zinedine Zidane) for the World Cup final. If we do not hold these moments in our memories, the show is left only to fan-shot DVDs and bootlegs. While those are well and good, they can only remind us of a time and place where, when the lights went down, we were all one voice to be heard and were all free to dream.

Private Show
Horseshoe Tavern
Toronto, Ontario
October 17th, 2006

It must be taxing for casual music fans to hang out with obsessed fans. It's impossible for casual fans to say they "like a song" without the obsessed going into a lengthy diatribe about the social ramifications of the song or rolling their eyes in a condescending, cooler-than-thou manner.

The rituals of the obsessed can be annoying, too. It doesn't matter that I love the bass line in "Greasy Jungle" and I often put it on once I hit my third or fourth beer of the night. It's an expression of emotion that can be aggravating, even for those close to me.

The problem then, is how obsessed fans can manage to enjoy themselves without ruining the night of whoever they are with. With the majority of Hip fans spread out across a continent and no weekly meetings to discuss our addictions, how can fans ever find each other, make meaningful connections and enjoy the show equally but for different reasons?

It's a wonder that those who *aren't* obsessed even go to gigs with me. It's even more of a wonder how bands themselves don't get annoyed with obsessed fans, especially if that fanbase is comprised largely of over-served dudes. (Rock and roll being an aphrodisiac, all-male bands that end up with mostly male fans must feel a little ripped off.) Between the constant chatter in my concert partner's ear and the between-song predictions of what's coming next (which are nearly always right), there's the shouting:

"FUCKING RIGHT! I HAVEN'T HEARD THIS SONG IN (insert incredibly short length of time)!"

"Check out (insert band member's name)! He's killing it!" (Known to casual fans as doing his job.)

And the kicker, which every obsessed fan has shouted at least once in their concert-going career: "Thank you! THANK YOU!"

Good manners have nothing to do with it. Obsessed fans shout "thank you" at concerts not because they want bands to know how much they appreciate their music, but because they *need* them to know. I shout "thank you" for the same reason I thank a bus driver. It would have been impossible for me to continue my day without his aid. The Hip, while they did indeed help shape my personality, also helped me get to where I needed to be, every day, during times when I was desperately seeking direction.

I shouted "thank you" throughout the Amsterdam '06 gig at the Paradiso. It's doubtful I would have experienced the visceral pleasures of one of the world's great cities had it not been for The Hip announcing a gig there during the end of my European odyssey.

After the show, our troupe of Hip followers waited outside the Paradiso eager to thank the band, but they never showed. Instead, Patrick Sambrook, their manager, came out and delivered the news: we weren't going to see them. The band was either going to stay inside the venue for some time, or were eager to slip out undisturbed into the Amsterdam night. It had been the greatest Hip gig I'd ever seen and I wasn't able to let the band know how I felt.

I took off, dejected, and soothed my pain with all the medicines that a Tuesday night in Amsterdam could provide.

The following evening, with the previous night's excesses still weighing on me, I stood front row at the Tivoli in Utrecht, waiting for the band to take the stage. Chris, the leader of our group, stood beside me, readying his video gear, eager to capture another night. Overcome with anxiety (as I am before every Hip gig), I stood staring at the stage. Chris broke the silence:

"Hey Joshua, after you left last night, we talked with Patrick some more," he said.

"Yeah?"

"He told us that even though the band wasn't coming out, they appreciated how far we had travelled."

"Okay?"

"He told us The Hip would be announcing some small club dates in Ontario in the fall and that all of us were guaranteed to be there!"

Though I'd only met Patrick for a few minutes, he

seemed like he knew exactly what to say to people in distress to make them believe that everything was going to be all right.

"Sounds cool," I offered.

I never believed anything would come of it. I thought anyone who attended a concert had to pay full price for a ticket, unless of course, they danced like a drunken buffoon in front of family members to win it. People like me paid for tickets, or got their parents to buy them, because that's what we did. I was not cool enough to go to gigs for free.

Less than three months later, I checked my email and read the following message from the band:

> *Hey Guys, I hope this finds you well. I would like to extend to you guys, a pair of tickets each, to the premiere of World Container on Oct. 17th at the Horseshoe Tavern in Toronto. Thanks again for your support of the band and everything that you have done and continue to do to promote the community and the music of The Tragically Hip. It does not go unnoticed.*

Patrick had kept his word. On October 17th, 2006, just a day before my twenty-third birthday, I would be attending a private, invite-only show at the Horseshoe Tavern to celebrate the release of *World Container*. Only days before, I had bounced around my apartment unable to contain my excitement over the impending release of the band's tenth full-length record.

I read the email a dozen times to make sure it wasn't a sick joke played on me by friends fed up with my incessant obsessive behaviour.

It wasn't. By this time, I'd begun writing for my university newspaper, interviewing touring bands and covering concerts, but being on a guest list was still a relatively new concept. And being on a guest list for a concert with

The Hip compared to a local pub night with a young band promoting their 7" single was akin to going from frozen, store-bought pizza to being flown to Naples, Italy for a slice of the real deal.

My girlfriend and I drove into Toronto and immediately became part of the elite: the people who bypassed those hordes of fans smoking nervously in the line. I didn't feel cocky; I felt like the whole thing was too good to be true. The Horseshoe is arguably the epicentre of music history in Toronto and the smallest venue in which I'd ever seen the band. To put things in perspective, the first time I saw The Hip, the venue was fifty-six times larger than the Horseshoe.

We still showed up a full two hours before the doors opened, just to ensure we'd get front row. I couldn't help but laugh as we gave our names at the guestlist booth, like we were a part of the "in" crowd. And when the band took the stage around nine o'clock, front row was where we stood.

The Hip have long been described as Canada's biggest bar band; their ability to pull off a grand performance in the smallest of venues has left many of their contemporaries in their dust. Well before the release of their self-titled debut EP in 1987, The Hip played the Horseshoe and showed a smallish crowd how far their chunky, blues-driven sound could stretch. It was at this very gig that MCA Records president Bruce Dickinson (yes, more cowbell) became so entranced by The Hip's live set that he offered them a multi-album deal.

Though The Hip's music was born in the basement of guitarist Paul Langlois's house long before that early gig, it learned how to speak at the Horseshoe Tavern. Twenty years later, I stood in front of bassist Gord Sinclair and marvelled at how things had come full circle. With the release of *World Container*, The Hip had brought their live set back to where it all began. I, too, had reached a pinnacle: I had been invited to a gig that, a year earlier, I would have given my every possession (except of course my beer-stained Hip jersey) to attend.

That night, I heard all eleven tracks from *World Container*, some of which the band played live for the first time. The Hip displayed the same amount of conviction that I'm sure they had twenty years earlier.

By "The Kids Don't Get It," the eleventh song of the night (and the most intense "The Kids Don't Get It" I've ever heard live), I was so engrossed in the atmosphere of the bar that I shook beads of sweat from my soaking hair onto Gord Sinclair's setlist. Onstage, it was all they could do to not bump into each other, not used to the cramped surroundings on a stage that so many young bands would kill for.

They made the best of it, interspersing classics like "Springtime in Vienna" and "Little Bones" with soon to be bona fide concert mainstays like "Family Band" and "The Lonely End of the Rink." I was there, not because I had danced like a loon the night before or because I had won a radio station promotion. I was there because I'd been with The Hip throughout my entire life as a fan.

I made eye contact with the entire band repeatedly that night. Still aware of my surroundings and that I was in a room I probably wasn't cool enough to be in, I screamed along to the words, and that was it. I didn't scream "thank you," because I knew everyone else was close enough to the band to have thanked them personally.

As they walked offstage after a riveting "The Wherewithal" (the second and last time I've heard the song played live) I smiled across the venue, still holding back the urge to thank the band while within earshot. The Hip had taught me so much, but they still hadn't taught me how to be cool.

Rob Baker, the last one to leave the stage, stuck his hand out. I shook it and the gig was over. I opened my clenched fist and found one of Rob's guitar picks in my palm.

Most of our troupe had hung back to capture the gig on video so that legions of fans could enjoy it in years to come. We all met on Queen Street afterwards, smoking and sharing the kinds of stories that only we would understand. Patrick Sambrook joined us, eager to hear what we had thought of the gig.

I stood dumbfounded. For years I had shouted "thank you," convinced my relationship was largely one-way. They gave, I received, and my life benefitted. But Patrick and a few other members of The Hip's team were so interested in our thoughts about the night and the new tunes that it felt wrong not to share. Of course, all I could muster up was "thanks for inviting me."

By the time Patrick left, it was nearly midnight. My girl told our group that I was about to turn twenty-three. Drunk, sweaty, and discombobulated on Queen Street, they serenaded me with an out-of-tune "Happy Birthday."

I was not with my friends, I was with people like me; people who realized the significance of the evening, people who knew that we would give our left arms for a band that didn't know our names. We are the ones who get a band to where they need to be.

I am not sexy or cool. Most obsessed fans forego these descriptors the minute they're able to wax poetic on a song that casual fans have never heard. But I have been there with the band, sometimes feeling light years away from them. I have stretched my arms out as wide as an ocean in an attempt to grasp their enlivening sound.

When the rag-tag group of singers finished, I looked at each of them and said "thank you."

"You're welcome," they said. It was one of those rare, perfect moments. We were a group of strangers brought together by a band. Turns out The Hip had heard my cries of "thank you" all along.

"[The Tragically Hip] always had that golden touch in terms of recognizing young Canadian talent and supporting that. I always saw that in them. They were clearly music fans. They wanted to take great bands like the Rheostatics, By Divine Right, Sam Roberts Band under their wing. They were so generous in that regard. I always remember feeling really down when we had to leave them and go back to playing shitty little clubs without them."

— Sammy Kohn, The Watchmen

CHAPTER 8

Revel in Discouragement and Failure

To truly love something you must also love its flaws. For some this love is one hell of a task, as any woman who has spent time with me would probably attest.

Never would I claim that The Hip are a "perfect" band. At times during gigs, Gord Downie's ragged voice loses harmonies and sounds akin to a wailing backwoods dog. Many of their songs end in dirty, blues-inspired solos. And to look at the band, there's nothing all that physically appealing about them. (It doesn't matter to me, but it's a valid argument.) Finally, having left the confines of Southern Ontario, I realize that the band doesn't give nearly as much touring love to the rest of the country as they do cities like Toronto and Hamilton.

Yet there's little that fans can do about any of that. The Hip's rough around the edges charm might not win over any new fans, but will definitely keep old ones for years to come. "Improving" The Hip's sound may not be possible, nor can I "improve" any of the downright embarrassing memories I have of the band. As much joy as they have brought me over the years, some of my memories are mired in shit.

There's no point letting these setbacks get you down. Yes, I've given up on bars after one bad night and given up on bands for the same reason. But if that philosophy dictated your entire life, you really wouldn't leave the house that often. Revelling in discouragement, failure, and embarrassment will only keep you coming back for more, if your love is strong enough. I suppose I should consider myself lucky that mine was.

◆◆◆

It's true that Gord Downie's voice can be stretched entirely too thin. There can be a pale ugliness to his voice, not unlike Neil Young's, that Hip fans identify with. Canadians have long eschewed clean, beautiful harmonies in exchange for a rugged charm that may very well represent the dirt under our proud fingernails. But what Downie lacks in vocal grace, he makes up for with his entire stage approach. He pushes it so hard that it's a wonder he makes it out of every gig alive. Sometimes, however, this pushing hampers the rest of the band. Paul Langlois's rigorous guitar-work is often overshadowed by Gord's intense stage presence. And when Downie flubs a lyric, it's not something that the entire band can laugh about and hide under a drum fill. It's the kind of let-down that haunts the next few songs of a set and stays with fans long after the last overpriced t-shirt is sold.

Though Toronto's Skydome has treated me to many unforgettable childhood sporting memories (Michael Jordan losing to the Raptors' during their inaugural year, the Blue Jays' march to their first World Series title), by 2003 I had never attended a gig there. The acoustics in the Skydome were legendarily awful so why I brought two skeptical Hip newbies to a gig there that year is beyond me.

I should have known better; this gig wasn't part of The Hip's tour. In the aftermath of the SARS epidemic that swept Toronto, a concert was scheduled to revive the city in one day. Promoters had to grab acts from across Canada's pop-music spectrum, including Avril Lavigne and the

Barenaked Ladies. Though they were all stars in their own right, the lack of musical cohesion throughout the day was palpable. It all came to a head during The Hip's set, which closed the evening.

I abandoned my post in the cheap seats, rushing down to the front and leaving my pals to fend for themselves. Closer to the stage, things got worse; the sound remained atrocious, but now I was exposed to the unnerving experience onstage. Downie butchered word after word, which threw off the band. Worst of all, it was a standard greatest-hits set. A big part of why Hip gigs are an exercise in joy is the spontaneity of the setlist. Massive screens broadcasted every glitch that happened onstage; I felt as if I were watching the show on television. I felt so disconnected from the band I knew.

A boring, predictable set, coupled with terrible sound, makes for a quiet ride home. This pillar of live rock and roll I'd believed in for years had been upstaged by Avril Lavigne. Though The Hip played the worst I'd ever seen that night, the terrible nature of the gig actually strengthened their stature as a live band.

Anybody can get lucky his or her first time doing anything. Let's put me, in all my wannabe rock glory, onstage with a few actual musicians. If our friends in the audience had the right amount to drink, we'd probably be able to pull a decent gig out of our hats.

The next day, we'd try it again after a few hours' drive in a cramped van. And that night would probably be our last as a live band.

It takes a lot for a band to play consistently well. Battling personal issues, fatigue and a poor diet, the good live bands do it every night. Great ones, like The Hip, can do it for many years. Yes, The Hip stank that night at the Skydome. But the band also played only three gigs that entire year, which is very telling.

Not only do The Hip tour consistently (in 2007, they

played over a hundred gigs, when the average age of a band member was forty-three), they harness the motion that is life on the road and channel it into their fluid and ever-changing sets. Being able to play together all the time is something that the band members are genuinely grateful for. As Rob Baker says in The Hip's behind-the-scenes DVD *Macroscopic*, "I get to make music with my friends. That's not work. It's a privilege."

Even the greats have off nights. And The Hip having an off night didn't do anything but increase my desire to see them. The Hip aren't just a live band, they're a road band. Day trips they don't do; long stretches into the great unknown are what form the backbone of the band and others of their ilk. And following on every lonely highway will be the dedicated fans, continually inspired by their reluctance to fade gracefully into the night.

◆◆◆

As a boy growing up in suburban Oshawa, there are a few rules that must be followed. They are:

1. Any reason is a good reason to rag on the Toronto Maple Leafs.
2. Anyone who complains about the cold has been beaten by the cold.
3. "Blue collar" is not an adjective; it's a way of life.
4. If you're going to leave Oshawa, make sure you have a damn good reason.
5. If you DO leave, stay true to the people you left behind.

Now, adhering to rule #4 but failing to abide by #5 is essentially grounds for high treason. Even if you plead guilty to this crime, as I have, you won't get a lighter sentence.

When I left Oshawa for university, I visited every month to regale old friends with massively embellished tales of sexual conquest. But eventually, Oshawa became less of a home to me, and leaving it behind meant exposure to a wider world. During the summer of 2004, I lived in a beaten-down university house and from there, departed for my first two American Hip road trips. It was my first summer away from Oshawa, and I haven't spent a long time there since.

But early in 2007, The Hip were booked to play Oshawa for the first time, in the city's new arena. I would return for the night with Jess and my sister. I anticipated an emotionally rewarding gig. I didn't feel awkward or nervous driving east on the 401 hours beforehand. I had come to make peace with my hometown, with The Hip there along the way.

Upon entering my childhood home, any chance of peace and tranquility disappeared. No one had left any messages wanting to meet for a beer. This gig could have happened if I wasn't there and nothing would have changed. The town I grew up in didn't give a shit about me.

So I got nervous. I stayed in my bedroom, drinking beer and watching *Seinfeld* reruns. By dinner, I was shit-faced. I felt the eyes around the table carving holes in me.

We left for the gig. It was up to The Hip to save the evening. This was a bit of misplaced pressure, but alcohol will always take the blame away from a confused young man returning home.

I walked the concourse of the General Motors Centre, looking for a familiar face. I was invisible. Ten minutes before The Hip would take the stage, I entered a crowded men's room. An old acquaintance towered above me. Amidst grunting, half-drunk GM workers pissing out their last beer, I froze.

"Hey Josh. Remember me?" he asked, his affable grin full of braces.

"Uh, yeah sure," I offered. I did remember him, but his name escaped me. It didn't seem like the most heinous of crimes.

"Oh yeah? Well, what's my name then?"

The entire arena was buzzing with anticipation, but inside that men's room, it seemed suddenly silent.

I fumbled. "I ah, don't, ah. Dude, wait, it'll come to me."

"You don't even remember my fucking name? We used to hang out. I voted for you for Student Council President in high school. What the fuck is wrong with you?"

I had no answer. After all, it was a great question.

He stormed out. A few of the husky drunks cursed at me under their breath. I returned to my seat, dejected. The Hip displayed their mastery that night, playing a punchy set full of blue-collar classics that they might have shied away from at different gigs. The crowd ate it up. The whole night, I battled both sadness and admiration: here was a band that knew how to adapt to a crowd. I had forgotten someone's name due to booze and shaky nerves, but my mistake felt amplified sitting there in the city that raised me. I had a lot to learn from those guys, including how not to piss on your hometown.

Instead of drinking myself into a stupor before the gig I should have looked to the last time the music of The Hip was so intertwined with my history in Oshawa.

A few years earlier, before I left to teach English overseas, a typically over-the-top party was thrown in my honour. All my old friends from Oshawa were there. (I'm not foolish enough to assume I was the only reason they came. Kegs and a live band generally trump a guest of honour.) Late that night, as my good friend's band, I'm With Stewy, treated the packed house to a number of cover tunes, I did my best to get in as many goodbyes as possible. The band played the intro to "Ahead by a Century," one of The

Hip's classics. My grinning friends stood in a circle around the band, imploring me to belt out the tune, for "old times' sake." The singer stepped away from the microphone, offering it to me.

But I refused. I couldn't sing it. Even through friends put me in headlocks, nothing could make me do it. Seeing as how Gord had long sang the song with a guitar in hand, it didn't feel right for me to work through my normal charade of his moves. The song was too important to me.

For me, Oshawa will always maintain a connection to "Ahead by a Century." The music video was shot north of the city, in the farming community of Brooklin. Two young lovers sit quietly and awkwardly in a single, large tree in a scene mirroring the awkward moments young lovers share in basements everywhere. It was a monumental video for The Hip, back when we watched videos on television. Tuning in at the right time and seeing the video was a big deal for a kid in Oshawa.

"Ahead by a Century" also holds a special spot personally. There's an extended jam that the band explores every time it's played live. I close my eyes and make a run for transcendence. Sometimes I am reminded of a lost love. Sometimes I let the inebriants really take hold. Or sometimes I remember how insanely talented this band is.

What has never occurred to me during that jam is that, though I've followed this band, I've mostly ignored the attitude that cemented their legacy. Born and raised in Kingston, most of the five members still live in the city. They're approachable and down-to-earth men. While waiting to talk to the band backstage, I've overheard numerous conversations they've had with friends from high school and the like. They support charities within the city, jam at local bars with smaller acts and employ artists from Kingston to design their cover artwork.

Their relationship with their hometown seems simple

and pure. That's a big reason why The Hip have maintained their popularity in Canada and especially in places like Oshawa. Some artists bring so much emotional baggage to the table that it becomes hard to relate to them as people. The Hip break down those barriers. Hip fans will attest: if they were to hire a band to play a large outdoor concert in the centre of their town, they'd call up The Hip. If they needed help putting shingles up on their roof, they'd probably call up The Hip. Dependable and loyal, The Hip's attitude towards their hometown is the polar opposite of mine.

When I listen to the jam in "Ahead by a Century," I'm a little too selfish, just like I am in most of my life. Looking back at that party, why couldn't I have realized that while the song was indeed important to me, my friends' memory of me singing the song at my going away party would have been *more* important?

The Hip will always remind me of home but represent my constant desire to push forward. So when they played "Ahead by a Century" that night in Oshawa's General Motors Centre, I closed my eyes and thought of that party and all those drunk, smiling faces. It would have been something we could have shared, long after I'd moved away. As the jam worked its way over the crowd, I tried desperately to make peace with my memories of my hometown.

◆◆◆

The highs and lows related to the band that fans experience are ultimately what separate them from society. When The Hip are on their game, everything else in my life just rolls along and there's no better feeling. But when the band lets fans down, people like me take things *personally*.

Many people assume that not only do I know every song word for word, I *adore* every song and lyric. But I'll be the first to admit that The Hip have released some real stinkers over the years. And to many, these are forgettable, skippable, non-downloadable tracks that are just sandwiched between the hits. But to people like me, they're faith-shaking. They're the reason that many of us always have our backs against the wall, ready to defend our band's art at the drop of the hat. So let's drop it.

DISAPPOINTMENTS IN THE HIP'S REPERTOIRE

"The Last Recluse" and "Coffee Girl"
We Are The Same
2009

I'll begin with not only one of The Hip's worst songs, but one of the worst songs I've ever heard. "The Last Recluse," a whiney folk ballad, manages to do the word "boring" a disservice. Not once does this song show signs of life. The meandering chorus, featuring a soft, timid Gord, asks the question: "Who are you-ou-ew?" I asked myself that same question of the band whenever it was played on rock radio after its release, which it frequently was.

The next track off *We Are The Same*, "Coffee Girl," is so boring it actually makes me physically angry. Opening with predictable drumwork, the song's smarmy adult-contemporary rhythm does little to get the blood flowing, yet it managed to find wide commercial appeal when it was released. It could have been the chorus, which might go down as Gord's single laziest lyric:

> "Hey there Coffee Girl/Beautiful and disaffected/
> It was perfect 'til/He came along and wrecked it"

The Hip have done their fair share of "love songs" in the past, but "Coffee Girl" pandered to a pop-leaning audience that had long ago rejected them. In fact, with the first spin of *We Are The Same*, something felt askew. These tracks occupy the meaty third and fourth spots on the record. As an album listener, the first and second tracks help you overcome the initial shock of hearing something new. You're now in for the long haul. The third and fourth tracks essentially make or break an album.

On previous Hip records, spots three and four have been reserved for outstanding combos such as "New Orleans is Sinking/38 Years Old" from 1989's *Up to Here* and "Ahead by a Century/Don't Wake Daddy" from 1996's *Trouble at the Henhouse.*

Yet these asinine tracks from *We Are The Same* were being marketed as singles, too. It all came to a boil six months after the record was released, when I heard "The Last Recluse" in a Chapters bookstore. I fled the magazines aisle to find Jess and get the hell out of there. She was grabbing a coffee in the adjacent Starbucks. With a wry, knowing smile, she handed me a "free download of the week" card. It was for "Coffee Girl." I didn't listen to the record again for weeks.

It wasn't that The Hip had "jumped the shark" and lost their creative edge. Somebody still thought the band had mass-market appeal, but neither of these songs possessed the sturdy and creative backbone of previous Hip tracks.

As the last tedious notes of "Coffee Girl" fade away, the band begins to show a free-flowing and jangly side. "The Depression Suite" starts as a loose and catchy track. Three minutes later, the song changes to a stompy, escalating number showcasing the band's grand side, with an especially poignant and now ironic chorus:

> "And I'm thinking, just in passing/What if this song does nothing?"

I was concerned that the entire record would do just that, but I was in for another shock. Two-and-a-half minutes later, the song shifts into its highest gear. With a heartfelt roll, the third part of "The Depression Suite" asks another more poignant question:

> "Don't you wanna see how it ends?/When the door is just starting to open?"

The Hip had tried meshing different songs together before, most notably with 2002's "The Dark Canuck." But "The Depression Suite" was different. It had scope and inspired possibility. The Hip were being daring and inventive again. Standing in the middle of the record, this nine-and-a-half minute composition is the glue that holds *We Are The Same* together.

Surely, something this inspiring deserved a bigger audience. But many friends skipped the track after four minutes. They wanted rock, but they sure weren't finding it on *We Are The Same*. A low-key, folky feel permeates the record, and though I'll agree it's one of their weaker efforts, "The Depression Suite" is the most engaging song they've released in the latter part of their career. It's just too bad they don't serve patience with coffee.

In Violet Light
2002

The Hip have written and recorded some mediocre songs. Only once did they produce an entire album full of them.

It took me a long time to realize what they'd done. Naturally, I didn't think it was possible. By 2002, I had a car, a great part-time job and an unabated desire to see the band. Had I been born five years earlier, I would have been able to apply this desire at (arguably) the height of the band's creative prowess and (definitely) the height of their popularity.

I was convinced that there was hidden beauty within each of the tracks on *In Violet Light* and that this was The Hip at their best, but this was only because I was now *really* on board. The reality is that the middle section of this record is home to a string of some of the worst material The Hip have ever given the world.

"It's a Good Life if You Don't Weaken" was the lead-off single. Although the band went to Oshawa to record the video, the song itself is like a river you sit and stare at for hours, searching for perspective, only to be left with nothing but a numb ass.

"Silver Jet" is the very definition of a generic rock song, with a sluggish beat and lyrics mirroring the track's pseudo-soaring nature. It's a song The Hip could have written in their sleep. To listen to the track now, it sounds and feels rushed and immature, as if the band were barely making an effort.

"Throwing Off Glass," an airy tune that lacks a punch, should have been relegated to a B-side. Heartfelt lyrics tell the story of a conversation between young and old, but musically, the song could cure the most restless insomniac.

"All Tore Up" sounds like the dim-witted cousin of "Silver Jet." The latter track already felt like a cheap rip-off of previous tracks, but to rip off tracks from the same album? All signs pointed to a band that seemed bored at the very idea of making records.

It pains me to say it, but things just weren't adding up back in 2002. That year, I managed to see the band six times over five months, and I was forced to hear these songs at almost every gig. Many took piss breaks for them. I stayed, singing along, trying to force a love for them.

"Leave" and "A Beautiful Thing" plod along without any efficiency or grace. "Leave" has only been played live four times, which says a lot for a Hip track. I'm not complaining, but when you consider that there are only two recorded Hip tracks that have never been played live, you get the sense that the band found nothing interesting about them.

In Violet Light was nearly saved by the tenth cut, the gorgeous seafaring tale "The Dire Wolf." I used this track in my last presentation in high school, a study of Alistair MacLeod's novel, *No Great Mischief.* Were it not for this gem, it would be tough for me to imagine even owning the album now.

By the last gig of 2002, a New Year's Eve celebration in Hamilton, I was so sick of hearing these tracks that even I began to take piss breaks for them. *In Violet Light* had great potential as a record, but one of the reasons it sounds "carefree" to the point of "not caring" might be because it was recorded in the Bahamas. The band's intentions were noble, but their output barely registers. To this day, only "It's a Good Life..." remains a mainstay in the band's live set. Thankfully, the door has closed on *In Violet Light*, but my doors were just opening in 2002. I was working hard to be a fan, spending enough money on tickets, gas, and food for these concerts to support a small country's economy.

Both the band and I shook off *In Violet Light* through 2003 and 2004. On June 29th, 2004, the band gave fans *In Between Evolution*, which stands as my third-favourite Hip record and their last classic. Concise and well-written, those thirteen tracks were the soundtrack to my first American gigs. It was a sure sign that the band was back to work, and I was ready to work alongside them.

The Majority of The Hip's Self-titled Debut EP 1987

Which of these pairs of lyrics from two different songs is the most resonant? "I lose control, I just can't stop/You look so good, like a big pork chop" and "Ripped my pants, ripped my shirt/I'm gonna eat your mother for dessert" or

"Building up to the larger point/With an arrogance not rare or pretty/We don't declare the war on idleness/When outside it's cold and shitty" and "We stay inside and try to conjure the fathers/Of the injured and faking/If there's glory in miracles/It's that they're reversible."

It's hardly a difficult choice. While only seven years separate the release of these lyrics, the writing quality is light-years ahead. The band doesn't play many of the songs from their EP live anymore. They're bland and soulless, synonymous with processed '80s rock. And with lyrics like the ones above from "I'm a Werewolf, Baby," The Hip sounded cheesy.

When discussing bands with a history, one of the most commonly heard observations is: "I don't mind them, but I like their early stuff better."

While this may be true for a lot of bands, with their self-titled EP, The Hip hadn't yet found their voice. Things began to pick up with 1989's *Up To Here*, but their EP was sonically and lyrically uninventive.

I don't win a lot of friends when I announce that the band's early records aren't what I hold most dear to me. A lot of people believe that's sacrilegious. But ask any Hip fan, or any music fan in Canada for that matter, to compare The Hip to another band. Very rarely will you get a comparison, and never will it be accurate. The Hip's early work is derivative of their musical inspirations, but by the mid-'90s, The Hip became their own inspiration. They crafted a sound all their own, and it's one that's fairly tough to replicate. A thousand adjectives have been used to describe it, but you can't use other bands as starting points. Adam Kasper, the producer of *In Between Evolution,* tried, and came close when describing the band: "If The Rolling Stones and R.E.M. were to have sex, the result would be a five-headed baby called The Tragically Hip."

He used two bands that also have a sound all their own.

What's worth noting (because fans note these things) is that both R.E.M. and The Rolling Stones sounded derivative on their first records. The Rolling Stones were a bar band that played blues standards and R.E.M. sounded like a '60s band whose approach was a little too strange for pop radio.

But a few albums into their respective careers, they started taking risks and the pay-offs were legendary, just as they were for The Hip. The band managed to fight through some fairly embarrassing early work and forge a career on their own sound.

On their first EP, The Hip were trying hard to be other bands. In a few years, The Hip managed to sound like The Hip, and only The Hip, without even trying.

"[The Tragically Hip] had this sort of Canadian 'nice' thing which was great because we were fans of the band. We shared labels and we shared the love of the same bands so we were loosely family in this thing. And Gord always impressed me as much offstage as he did onstage in terms of being hyper-present, articulate and me being just a little bit intimidated by that. But I also wanted to be around him because he was the real deal in a way that I don't usually have access to people."

— *Ryan Miller, Guster*

CHAPTER 9

Travel for the Band

The idea of travelling to "find oneself" has been beaten into an embarrassing cliché, though it exists for a reason: eventually, most travellers will admit to it at least once.

The freedom to become someone new is tempting for those unhappy with the lives they're leading. People who leave their homes happy with who they are, and return home equally happy, aren't travellers so much as vacationers. The difference is ocean-sized.

Travelling to see The Hip felt like more of an inevitability than a choice for me. My love of the band had grown larger than suburban Southern Ontario, the tiny world I called home. There was nowhere else for my obsession with The Hip to go but out into a world I barely understood.

Of course, I *wanted* to see The Hip in different locales. When the notion first entered my head in the summer of 2004, it set up shop in my psyche and refused to be evicted. Travelling for the band not only fed my obsession, but reminded me of what *Fully Completely* had implanted in me years before: the desire to move and the desire to find.

◆◆◆

Places like Paris or India are romanticized and idealized with a degree of ease. Over the years, The Hip introduced Canadians to the beauty and idealism in their own backyards, as well as giving Canadians the opportunity to see the world around them and better define their own place in it.

I would read about their tours as a kid, learn their setlists and look up the capacity of the small-town hockey rinks they'd play—for no real reason other than my genuine desire to be part of something. And even as a kid, I knew if I was going to be a Hip fan, simply playing the CDs and memorizing the lyrics wasn't enough: I would have to find this band not in venues like Toronto's Air Canada Centre, but in the rest of the world that The Hip so constantly referred to.

Darien Lake Performing Arts Center
Buffalo, NY
July 23rd, 2004

The Hip and Canadiana go together as well as pancakes and maple syrup. But I wanted to see just what sort of affect this band would have on me south of the border. And only having been to the USA on vacations with my parents, it was time for me to travel alone, with the thing I loved most in the world giving me the confidence to see if I could even survive outside of my tiny home.

On a Friday afternoon, I travelled to Buffalo with three other Hip fans, only one of whom I'd met before. I'd seen the band just three weeks earlier, a fact of which everyone around me was aware.

In coming to terms with my obsession and the reality that this obsession was able to stretch across borders, it felt like everything I did broke some sort of law.

The three Hipheads went out of their way to pick me up in Guelph. We drove the two-and-a-half hours to the venue and talked of nothing but the band. I didn't learn a single thing about the personal lives of those three guys; why would we have fooled ourselves into thinking we cared about such information?

As we pressed through the border, I realized how different this gig was going to be. At shows I'd attended with friends, the show itself became an integral part of our relationship. But with the Darien Lake gig, the obsession was already a shared one. For each of us, it was our first American show. This gig wasn't for us as a whole, but for each of us personally. That was the first of many small differences I'd notice that day. While travelling, it's the little things that carry the most weight.

Walking through the dusty, makeshift parking lot we heard a low, distant rumbling. As we got closer to the actual amphitheatre, the rumble became the bass line to "Chagrin Falls," a rarely heard cut from 1998's *Phantom Power*. The four of us stopped as we silently realized that we were all losing another aspect of our Hip virginity: our first soundcheck.

We ran to the back of the amphitheatre and pressed our ears against the old, rickety wooden boards that separated us from our heroes. The walls were too tall to climb and lifting each other up would have blown our cover. We were after all, trying to play it cool in this strange, exotic place. What was a regular part of the band's day provided us with a foreign, wicked reward. We weren't doing anything wrong, but being away from our normal "Hip home" felt so exciting and so evil at the same time.

Inside the venue, sitting patiently in our seats twenty rows back from the stage, I got an idea of how different this amphitheatre was from the one I'd been to for two gigs in 2002 (the Canada Day gig three weeks earlier and a Pearl Jam gig that still ranks in my top five of all time). Darien Lake had the rustic charm of a small-town ballpark; a stark difference from the polished and slightly impersonal feel of

Molson Amphitheatre in Toronto, the venue I'd become so comfortable with.

Finally, the show. The band had a patient approach, mocking my eager enthusiasm. They allowed their songs to stretch and find their legs. Considering the nature of the trip, it was hard for me to stay in my seat during "Vaccination Scar," the driving opener. Two songs later, I went to the nearest barrier ten rows back from the stage and asked the security guard if I could take a few photos. When he replied, the affability of what seemed like the entire crowd shone through:

"Hell, for all I care, you can go right to the front!"

He barely got the words out before I made a rush for the stage, eager to see the front row for the first time. When I got there, without hassle, and stood in a vacant spot, the band was working their way through "Grace, too." My entire body was tingling. I was silent. I snapped photos and watched in awe as the band performed only feet away from me. In the twelve gigs I'd seen before this one, I'd never managed to actually *see* the band's faces. The closer I got, the scarier things felt, like a fire blazing out of control. I had left my backyard and now I had a front-row seat to the circus.

In the days leading up to the gig, I had had nightmares of being so close to the stage that I could feel the sweat dripping from the band, yet had forgotten my camera and had no way of documenting the occasion. Read into that dream what you will, but what remained was my desire to travel for the band, and my fear that that desire would become satiated after just one gig.

I could never go back to massive stadium shows now. They had only tempted me. It wasn't just that I'd discovered a new venue. This gig had given me a new way to see the band and appreciate them in an entirely new light.

As the band wrapped up a seven-and-a-half minute version of "Grace, too," the rightful owner of the seat showed up and gave me hell. I returned to my seat nineteen rows back, but the damage was done. On my first "Hip trip," I had seen the Promised Land. The differences between setlists that summer might have been small, but the impact was large.

The first venture into any unknown land, big or small, is a dramatic one. I rode home in the back of a sedan with the inescapable images of the band, unobstructed, dancing in my head.

◆◆◆

For Hip fans, travelling has always been a sacred duty. The band has played countless cities and towns in Canada alone. They have never stood still; they're egalitarian enough to play towns that rarely see touring bands. The road is a vehicle for The Hip, like all great rock and roll outfits.

"We play wherever we can; be it on the ass of an elephant," Gord Downie once said.

Touring is so emotionally exhausting that it becomes difficult to understand its importance. Bands like The Hip do all the work and the fans do all the escape. The band allows people who spend their lives behind desks or putting up drywall to step into a venue that may have been empty the night before and create a memory they can return to when stuck back at their day job. Not everyone is blessed with the talent to paint, play an instrument, or sing, but a concert allows everyone, from factory workers to wide-eyed students, to find a place that is both transitory and transformational. The music itself disappears quite quickly, but any band worth its salt will show up and give its fans permanent memories.

The great rock and roll bands get addicted to this lifestyle, even if they don't *need* to be, financially speaking. But there is an explicit give and take that happens on the road between the band and their fans that keeps the train rolling. Some fans are happy to ride the train once, just to say they've done it. By the time I was twenty-one, I was ready to be the goddamned engineer.

Fillmore East
Irving Plaza
New York, NY
April 24th and 25th, 2007

New York City exists for many as a mirage within pop culture. As a place, it always seems impossible to get to. And even when you arrive, it's as if there's always a little further you have to go to find what you're looking for. No one fully understands the city, which is probably the biggest part of its allure.

Like most people who'd ever turned on a television, I had wanted to see New York City for a long time. At first, the city seemed intimidating; when I decided to travel there alone via overnight bus for the sole purpose of seeing The Hip on their *World Container* tour, I feared the possibilities.

I had just finished my last year of university and couldn't shake the idea of seeing New York City for the first time. The events surrounding the gig had convinced me. Having just finished my last batch of exams, I was heading for another mundane summer of work in Guelph and was set to leave for a job in Istanbul come September. This trip to NYC had infinite potential. Part of me felt like I'd been working towards it.

Perhaps my determination was due to Constantines, a young, gritty band out of Guelph who would be opening for The Hip in New York City. I'd been following them with interest for a few months. They were much younger than The Hip but their earthy aesthetic had me grooming them as possible replacements long down the line.

The Hip's respect for their opening acts is palpable.

They handpick young Canadian bands to showcase their tunes to an audience that otherwise might be oblivious. I feel a kinship with opening bands; my lone flirtation with musical success occurred as an opener.

◆◆◆

In 2005, while teaching in Poland, I was given the chance to open for the house DJ at a nightclub on a Saturday night and get paid in booze. Before the doors opened, I looked at the empty dance floor from my booth perched ten feet above it. It dawned on me: with all this opportunity, why not just "will the crowd into it" and make it impossible for the house DJ to follow me?

A gracious group arrived early and grew accustomed to my Canadian-centric set. Soon they were dancing to tunes they'd never heard before. I couldn't stand still myself, dancing and soaking up my payment. It was Saturday night and only the coat check girl wasn't moving.

The gracious house DJ brought me pint after pint. An hour into my set, the dance floor was packed. I had made a move for the bathroom fifteen minutes in, but even with the five-minute track I'd tossed on, I had barely made it back in time.

Torn between excitement and responsibility, I kept drinking. The booze was working, but so was the evening. I tallied five empty pint glasses in my first hour. Riding an untouchable high, I gave into temptation and played "Poets," my first Hip song of the evening. The energy took hold; as Rob Baker led the band through the outro jam, I caught the coat check girl busting a move. I am reminded of her every time I hear the song.

I continued to up the tempo and kept draining glasses. Ninety minutes in, somewhere inside a Sam Cooke number, I realized if I didn't get to a toilet, I would explode with Żywiec, Poland's finest lager. Leaving would mean having to play a longer number. The momentum I'd built would be dead on the table. As I twitched in agony, the house DJ gave me my ten-minute warning. Ten minutes. Six hundred seconds. Waiting was impossible; I was pacing like a caged lion. I gave into temptation again. The crowd needed something to remember me by, so I spun "Thugs," a Hip tune I'd never heard live. The crowd fell into the trance of the bass-heavy groove as their pace slowed and their bodies grew closer. I felt calm and took stock of the evening: a success.

But I had waited a second too long. With the bathroom line-up now snaking out the door, I stood in the booth and cemented my DJ'ing legacy by pissing my pants. I froze then began to laugh hysterically. Thousands of kilometres away from home, I pissed my pants with The Hip in the background. Depending on how many aspiring Canadian DJs with a love for '90s homegrown rock would roll through the city of Wrocław, I reckoned this would be the last time anybody in the crowd would ever hear "Thugs." My shoes began to soak up the urine and I waved the house DJ over. I'd done my part: I'd introduced a foreign crowd to The Hip and flirted with greatness. Some bands only get one shot opening for the big boys and worry so much that they forget to let loose. You have to leave your mark, regardless how important the headliner.

I gave the DJ a high-five and crawled down the ladder. The last thing I saw was him sniffing with a strange look on his face, unsure of what had happened to the stage he'd long called his own.

◆◆◆

I wandered throughout New York City on my first day. While the city is a great place to be aimless, nothing celebratory or monumental happened.

I arrived at the venue a few hours before the doors opened to soak up some excitement and a few drinks. There,

I met two guys from Halifax who had arrived under circumstances similar to mine; having finished their last year of university, they flew in just for the show. Like me, they felt compelled to come to New York City for these gigs, but they too had wandered the streets all day without a purpose.

The doors opened and we hugged the rail in the front row, eager to see our favourite band in the centre of the universe. There was no debate: this could very well be the most important gig of our lives.

While Gord has gone on record saying that "for a show to be great, something has to happen," that doesn't leave fans with much in the formula department. So if a band, even an opener, *wants* a great show badly enough, odds are they might just get one. It's something that Constantines understood. They took the stage aware of the enormity of opening for the greats in New York City. Their set was uncompromising. The Hip would come onstage afterwards and play a healthy set, but there was no touching Constantines. It was the only time I've ever seen The Hip bested by the opening act.

Afterwards, sitting outside drinking Mountain Dew and smoking cigarettes, my companions and I tried to rationalize what had happened. All three of us had expected too much. The Hip didn't seem to be influenced by their surroundings to the extent that we were. Absent from the set were the band's two songs referencing New York City: "Escape is at Hand For the Travellin' Man" ("It was our third time in New York/It was your fourth time in New York/We were fifth and sixth on the bill") and "Flamenco" ("Maybe I'll go to New York/I'll drag you there/You said 'No one drags me anywhere'").

They played a cover song I'd never heard before, one that no one I spoke to could identify either. My dreams of hearing a Ramones or a Lou Reed cover were left unrequited.

To make things even worse, as the three of us stood outside the venue, wondering how to glean something from the city, Rob, Johnny, and Gord Sinclair passed us, clearly en route to an after-party. We tripped on our tongues; instead of trying to tag along, we couldn't offer much more than a "good show."

Minutes later, Richard Beland, The Hip's official photographer, passed us. I'd met him a year earlier in Europe. He invited us along to the after-party, but we declined. It was apparent that we were all waiting for a word with Gord Downie, though no one wanted to admit it. Beland shrugged and continued on. Not twenty minutes later, we snapped out of the stoned grip NYC had on us and decided to haul ass over to the pub where the after-party was being held.

Through the window of the pub we saw Beland having a laugh with Rob. The bouncer wasn't having any of us. "Private party," he said. Defeated, we went our separate ways and hoped for more from both The Hip and ourselves the next night.

Back at my hostel, I escaped to the rooftop patio and passed out in confusion just before daybreak. Perhaps New York City is the city that never sleeps; I couldn't help but wonder if those who stayed awake had a better idea of what they were looking for.

◆◆◆

I spent most of the next day walking through Central Park with a Swedish artist I'd met in the hostel. After I told her I was following a band, she regaled me with tales of her time following a band much younger than The Hip. She never asked exactly who I was following, and in retrospect, I'm glad she didn't.

Our conversation turned rather serious, as talks with strangers in parks can tend to. She shared her insights on how clueless parents could be when it came to their children's desires, and confessed that it was hard for her to trust people much older than her. I'll always remember what she said:

"Surely, they don't understand. People become so out of touch when their generation is replaced by a generation younger than them. I really don't believe there is any way that young and old can see eye to eye."

"Just how old are you talking here?" I asked.

"Anyone over forty."

It left me rattled. I had been travelling for a band that had been making music together for as long as I'd been alive. How long would I make these trips? I thought about Constantines, a younger band that had blown The Hip out of the water the previous night. Had I fallen out of touch with my own peer-based culture, as I had years ago, forsaking punk for classic rock? New York City wasn't giving me any answers.

In high school, the world seemed so grand and fascinating. Throughout university, the world became small enough to be possible. Now, I was done with both, alone in one of the biggest cities on Earth. My obsession, which had stuck by me through both high school and university, had let me down. It had been upstaged by youth.

This wasn't just the usual self-pity and longing for companionship that occasionally plagues solitary travellers; this was confusion of the most genuine and startling kind.

I wandered for hours before ending up in the East Village. I walked by a mural of Joe Strummer painted on a wall and stared at it, transfixed. Tourists wandered by, snapping photos. I had to read the simple four-word inscription over a dozen times before I actually processed it:

"The future is unwritten."

I raced back to the hostel and searched my iPod for *Global A Go Go*, the debut record from Joe Strummer and the Mescaleros. I'd bought the record years earlier but had never given it more than a few listens. I was sitting on the rooftop again when "Johnny Appleseed" came on. I now recognized the track The Hip had covered the night before. My visit was beginning to have purpose. The longer one is a fan, the more difficult it becomes to attain a thrill. After all, fans have seen it all before. It felt good to enjoy the simple pleasure of hearing a new song and connecting the dots.

Thank you, New York City. I finally had my moment.

Naturally, The Hip recovered by working tirelessly and laying down a classic set that night. So hard did the band work to churn out a comprehensive and cohesive set that members of Constantines were spotted taking pictures in awe.

Afterwards, I found Richard Beland and talked him into a few drinks. Many beers later, I confessed that his job, following and documenting bands across the world, was a dream of mine.

He laughed politely, but stopped when he met my serious, pleading stare. I confessed that the life he led seemed like an impossibility for me. We stared into our drinks; he began what sounded like a standard reply. I continued to stare into him and he stopped mid-sentence.

"Wait, did you just say you *just* graduated university?" he asked.

I nodded.

"Joshua, you have so much time. Believe me. Just enjoy what you're doing right now."

Just over a year later, on my way home from the Middle East, I would visit New York City again. Since The Hip weren't touring through any major flight hubs at the time, I had timed my return to coincide with Pearl Jam's concert at Madison Square Garden.

During a powerful version of "Rearviewmirror," I committed the cardinal sin and left for the men's room. I struggled to open my fly as the floor beneath me bounced up and down, and accidentally pissed on my shorts, another New York City moment. I zipped up and smiled, partly because of what I had done, but also because I knew this would not be the last time loud music would inspire embarrassment. Though I had just landed, my desire to re-immerse myself was strong. Right after the show, I'd board an overnight bus home, rest for two days, and then take another bus headed for Ottawa, where The Hip were playing the Ottawa Bluesfest. I'd been away for way too long.

New York City, one of the greatest cities on Earth, made me realize an eternal truth of travelling: the journey is the destination.

European Tour
July 5th-12th, 2006

Like many others, it took me a while to figure out exactly how I was going to make a living. I'd had some unique career goals when I was young. "Fighter pilot" and "host of *Sportscentre*" are two that I'm proud of, though my brief detour into politics is certainly a blemish. But of all the professions I considered in my youth, there is only one that I regret not pushing a little harder for.

As the adage goes, "music critics are just failed musicians" and like many other critics, I am always trying to make the annoying voice in my head sound like the coolest person in the room. I didn't want to be a musician, though; I wanted to be in a band. And yes, there's a huge difference: just ask Bill Wyman.

The thought of a life lived on the road, with all its bad food, alcohol, and poor personal hygiene still makes me stare away from my computer wistfully.

Sure, I could never play an instrument. Hell, I had a hard enough time in my fifth-grade music class mastering "every good boy deserves fudge." I never had the patience for an instrument, but that wasn't the real reason my dream failed: I couldn't sing.

I wanted to sing. I wanted to be the frontman. My fondness for Gord Downie's perplexing lyrics and twisted stage presence were the initial pieces of the puzzle. I'd read the liner notes with an impassioned search for truth that I never showed in seventeen years of schooling. I even began reading poets and writers that Downie was influenced by as a means to improve my own poetry. But I wasn't kidding anyone; I wasn't a poet, I just wanted to sing. I wanted to stand in front of a crowd and feel the warmth that I directed at the stage at every Hip show.

Singing karaoke, the next best thing, would always produce the same results: I'd try and sing the first verse (always a Hip tune, mind you) with passionate sincerity. The entire bar would cringe. And almost on cue, I'd start mocking Gord's moves and his stream-of-consciousness rambling. The cringes would turn to laughter, and I'd have the entire bar in the palm of my sweaty, shaking hand. I wasn't an entertainer, because all true entertainers are original. It was a bar trick. And although I had always wanted to be part of an original rock and roll band, my obsession with The Hip's music and everything it shares a kinship with (Al Purdy's poetic, bar-room drawl, the grandiose but honest aesthetic of Pearl Jam's arena rock and finally, the purity and hardship of the Delta blues) ultimately outweighed my ability to create my own original lyrics.

I was forever destined to be a rock and roll "fan." I made my comfortable, queen-sized bed in a house with a fridge, good-enough speakers, and a warm body beside me. And now I lie in it, instead of lying on a cold floor, broke and hungry, with a few hundred kilometres to drive to the next show.

Though my ambitions were quashed, my curiosity

wasn't. Through interviewing bands, I've learned that one of the most common reasons bands break up is their inability to deal with "life on the road." After hearing this a few times, I wondered: Is the dream harder to maintain than I'd originally thought? Would I even be able to handle the lifestyle of a touring musician?

◆◆◆

Late January, 2006. The coldest day of the year in Wrocław, the Polish city I had been calling home for six months. The wind was so strong and the flurries so blinding that I began to get scared sitting alone in my apartment. I put on every piece of clothing I owned and trudged to the comfort of the internet cafe. I needed the warmth of familiarity; the shitty weather had me wallowing in self-pity. Was moving to Poland a mistake? Why was I living in a city that was just as cold as Canada, but without any of the comforts of home?

Between pathetic emails to friends, I checked out The Hip's fan-based message board hoping for rumours about a new record. The band had been largely inactive for the past year. When I saw that there was a new tour date announced, I assumed it was in Toronto, and felt even more jealous of Southern Ontario.

But when I read that the band was playing Amsterdam in July, at the legendary Paradiso, I felt light-headed and warm, despite the cold. The gig was only a few months away. It was a reason, a purpose, to stay away from home.

Over the next few weeks, a five-date Western European tour was finalized. The chance to test my road legs was upon me. I knew by the time the tour arrived I'd be feeling the strain of a year of drinking and low pay, which would definitely lend my road experiment some credibility. I began counting down the days.

◆◆◆

As I walked to the Wrocław train station at dusk, I imagined a band leaving home for their inaugural tour. I had to believe that this tour of mine was the most important thing in the world I could be doing. If you embark on any adventure believing otherwise, there's no real point in going.

My enthusiasm came to a halt as I waited outside Katowice's small airport (so small it closed overnight) until the doors opened at sunrise. Maybe this wasn't *supposed* to be fun. Maybe if I wanted to sample the lifestyle of a touring band, I would have to accept the fact that the road is a bumpy one.

I finally boarded a small aircraft and waves of anticipation returned. I could hardly sit still. The departure time came and went. The plane sat motionless on the runway. The passengers were soon asked to leave the plane, as it was unfit to fly.

Back inside the airport, the minutes turned to hours. I paced endlessly. Unknown variables are hard on the superstitious and obsessed. I had to be patient, but when you're used to everything going according to plan on the day of a gig (from the departure time, to the kind of beer consumed, to the songs when I would light a cigarette), this first "tour" of mine was already in trouble. If it kept up, my nervous and giddy nature might eat the sane, relaxed part of my brain for a mid-flight snack.

By the fifth hour of the delay, I pleaded with a clueless attendant at the information booth for more details about my flight. I lent him my headphones and cued up "Fireworks."

"I'm on my way to follow this band through Europe," I said.

"It's pretty good," he offered in stilted English. Still, he had no idea when the flight would depart.

While emotion drives all great art, touring requires a stone-cold state of mind. Paradoxically, the emotion that most obsessed fans identify with is anticipation. We scour fan sites endlessly in the months before a record-release date, trying to match new songs heard on the last tour with possible titles. We log onto ticket-brokering websites hours early and click "refresh" thousands of times, waiting for the "on sale" logo to appear. And the long moments between the opening band walking offstage and the lights going down again are usually enough to send obsessed fans into near-cardiac arrest.

Finally, after nine hours of pacing the Katowice airport, I was in the air. And after a brief flight I was checking into my hostel in London, just a short walk from Shepherd's Bush Empire, the first venue of the tour. I wandered down into the hostel bar for a few drinks.

I sat in a corner of the bar, staring at a group of men whose neutral Canadian accents nearly brought tears to my eyes. They wore matching homemade grey t-shirts with a line from "Puttin' Down," a deep cut from *Music at Work*:

> "There's reasons for the road, I guess/To document the indigenous"

I knew this tour would be filled with displaced Canadians, many of whom would give weight to the argument that Hip fans are a barbarous bunch. But as I listened to these fans, I knew that their drinking was only fueling their enthusiasm, not any indecency.

After making my way over to the table, Chris (of Cleveland and Detroit fame) greeted me with surprise and shock and introduced me to the rest of his troupe. It didn't take long before I was sharing in their buckets of Corona and rejoicing at our accidentally finding one another. All our differences—age, marital status, weight—were irrelevant. This was the first time that any of us had followed The Hip abroad, and for many of them, their first trip overseas.

Our anticipation grew with every bucket of Corona. This ritual *had* to happen. We had to get to know each other before we travelled across three countries together. There was a feeling that couldn't be contained. We just knew that this tour would lead to great, unforeseen things. Somewhere around our seventh bucket, we wondered why the sounds of the band couldn't accompany us while we drank. I darted up to my hostel bunk bed without another word.

Some people wear crosses around their necks for protection. Others carry photos of loved ones in their wallets as a reminder of what is good and pure in this world. During my time in Poland, I carried around *Live Between Us* for much of the same reasons. The band's lone live record held such emotional weight for me I would feel nervous if it weren't constantly within reach. I'd use it to turn others onto the band, listen to it in times of desperate homesickness, or just flip through the liner notes as a reminder of the world that was waiting for me.

Now, the two worlds I lived in had collided. When the bartender obliged my request to play the record, our group of seven collectively lost our shit. We danced as if no one was watching (which was the truth, as we had emptied the bar of all other patrons) and connected two strange worlds: the comfortable and the foreign.

It wasn't just a geographical connection. We were relying on each other to hold ourselves up, far away from home. We didn't know each other, but now we were all in this discovery together.

We stood and punched the air emphatically as "Twist My Arm" came to its driving close and felt a collective spirit that separated us from other fans. None of us could play guitar, but our desire and commitment to the task at hand made us, if only for one driving end to a classic song, more than just fans. From different cities but with our goals now common, in our eyes, we had become a band. And we wanted the tour to begin.

◆◆◆

The next night we were the first in line outside Shepherd's Bush Empire. I went so far as to sit down and lean against the old wooden doors that led into the club. After an hour of waiting I felt a nudge at my back. Five months of anticipation were about to end. I threw my ticket at the doorman and *ran* to the front row. I grabbed the rail and refused to let go.

When the lights went down, my usual feeling of weightlessness didn't arrive. Instead, I was remarkably grounded. The Hip sauntered onstage with massive smiles and I didn't say a word. Gord Downie grabbed the microphone stand and gave the crowd his standard, sweeping greeting:

"Hello."

He waved. In a daze, I looked behind me for the first time and saw the grand old theatre, packed with rabid fans. No more worries about whether or not this tour was too good to be true. No more flight delays. Just the gigs. I'd kept a promise I'd made to myself. I'd have paid every bar tab in London that night if I didn't have to leave the front. Holding that rail meant I wouldn't be pulled away from exactly where I seemed destined to be.

The band started slow, opening with "Don't Wake Daddy," a shuffling grower of a tune. The winding bass line along with Johnny Fay's penetrating drumwork hit me. I had made it through a year abroad, alone. I hadn't seen The Hip live in a year-and-a-half, and now I stood front-row centre, on the other side of the Atlantic Ocean.

As the song continued to grow, my intentions became clear. I snapped out of my trance. If I really was on tour, then it was time to do *my* job. I may not be in the band, but for the two hours the band is onstage, it's my job to keep them afloat.

So I sang along. I wore a shit-eating grin for two hours, pointing at each band member when they would go above and beyond the call of duty. I did the things I'd always wanted to do as a fan, but always felt slightly restrained. This gig had all the emotional and geographical elements to make it special. Not only had I survived a year alone, I had survived a year away from the one thing that made home a slightly attractive place to be.

When I decided not to extend my contract in Europe and return home to finish my last year of school, I sent an emotionally revealing email to my parents. I ended on a lighter, but truthful note. I told them that I had to come home for 2006-2007 because all signs were pointing to a new Hip record in the late summer and an impending Canadian winter tour.

Seeing The Hip in London reminded me not only how important this band was to me, but how important it was for me to be a fan. I realized that once a band graduates from the basement and makes their first true fan, one cannot live without the other. I embraced my role and sang louder than I ever had.

◆◆◆

Before the last night of the tour on July 12th, I began to feel good about who I was and what I had learned during my year abroad. And, as young adults are prone to do, I got cocky. Insisting to myself I had a leg up on an entire ocean, I assumed that that evening's show at Tivoli in Utrecht would be as memorable as my first. And in many ways, it was.

On the afternoon of the show, my nerves started to get the best of me. I ran into Billy Ray, The Hip's musical equivalent of a knight in shining armour. As long as I've been a fan, Billy Ray has been The Hip's go-to stage hand, sporting a well-worn black leather cowboy hat that hangs over his face, hiding his smug grin. He stood by a canal, smoking Canadian cigarettes. I'd only started smoking during my time in Poland, so Billy Ray and his stubby cigarettes reminded me of the students I'd see smoking in high school who used to make me nervous and awkward.

I hesitantly approached him. Midway through our brief conversation, he told me that the band had to leave for a flight immediately after the gig and return to Canada. He slid this into the conversation so subtly that I didn't really think about it.

As the minutes clicked away outside the Tivoli, I reflected on my previous three years at school, the ones that I'd been lead to believe were "the best of my life." Entire weeks had gone by where nothing of remote consequence occurred. As memorable as nights spent hot-boxing a bathroom or days spent jumping off roofs might have been, I was just going through the motions and I doubt I was alone.

But this one week had been the culmination of a year spent becoming the kind of person I'd always envied. As the doors to the Tivoli opened, I looked out over the canals of Utrecht and its affable citizens biking by. I would be returning to Canada and the life I left behind in a matter of days, but the person I would be once I got there depended entirely on how much of the past year I could stuff in my backpack and bring back with me.

◆◆◆

The band appeared on the tiny stage. I gazed at my once-mythological heroes. Throughout the past week that I'd spent in close quarters with the band, they'd gone from untouchable giants to mere mortals. And if I was after fitting endings, then I was about to be served five-courses of reality.

From the opening drum beat of "Don't Wake Daddy," something felt off. Hip gigs have always been timeless in that the world outside the venue ceases to exist. But at the Tivoli, the band looked and sounded as if their collective conscience was elsewhere.

Paul looked lethargic, strumming his guitar carelessly. He lacked the punchy drive that usually propelled "Courage." Directly in front of me, the usually consistent Gord Sinclair and Rob Baker had no chemistry. "Daredevil" rolled along limply.

Midway through the set, I became angry. Why was the band treating this gig like any other? Why didn't they realize that this gig was something I would take with me on a flight across the Atlantic, where I would desperately try to come to terms with the rest of my life? I was angry enough to keep my hands in my pockets after a lifeless "Yer Not The Ocean," in which Gord's frustration began to show. He pleaded with the sound crew to fix the atrocities onstage, but there was no helping the gig.

"At The Hundredth Meridian" popped up mid-set, as it often does. The barnburner of a song cannot only rescue a routine Hip gig, but propel a good gig into a legendary one. I prayed that the roaming fury of the track might save the night. Instead, during the song's crescendo, Downie kicked at one of the grey shirt's cameras with his foot. Intentional or not, he was sending a clear signal: this was one night that did not deserve to be documented.

By the fifteenth song of the evening, I had all but given up. Then, during the slow, building intro to "Escape is at Hand For the Travellin' Man," I began to see the light. Throughout my year in Europe, this song had been a crutch. Its rumbling momentum had helped me through gloomy Polish winter mornings and encroaching bouts of homesickness. Downie strummed furiously as the song picked up steam. It wasn't the momentum that was fuelling his strumming, but growing frustration with the sound quality of the evening. He'd reached his breaking point. Taking off his acoustic guitar and throwing it to the ground in anger, Downie showed fans a side we had always feared existed: like the rest of the world, The Hip have bad days and their frustration hits a boiling point.

When the band reappeared for an encore, Downie thanked us "for sticking around." Perhaps he thought there were better things we could be doing with ourselves that evening after the band's awful performance. Or maybe he was thanking the crowd that had been with the band, not only during that week in Europe but throughout their whole career. His admission of guilt on behalf of the band was the most memorable part of the show.

Ups and downs are an inevitable part of every job. With most jobs however, you can walk away from a bad day, have a drink, complain to your significant other, and no one is the wiser. But with touring bands, whose fans sometimes wait years to see them live, a disappointing gig can echo for years to come.

The band finished with a standard "Fireworks." Gord thanked the crowd again and told us to have a wonderful summer. The rest of the band offered meagre smiles and a few waves then disappeared behind the stage. The blinding house lights came up. I had woken from the dream that had been the last year of my life.

My experience and the band's experience were oceans apart. I had left Canada with few emotional ties. But the country I had left in excitement was the country to which the band could not wait to return. In Canada, The Hip had wives, families, and friends that depended on them. I waited outside the venue after the show and shook a few hands, though for the most part the band slid into a waiting van and disappeared into the Utrecht night. It was all I could do not to plead with them as they brushed me off. I wasn't part of the paparazzi, yet I was still a distraction. I had to accept the fact that as much as The Hip had mattered to me that week, the feeling was not mutual.

◆◆◆

I had worked during my time abroad, but as anyone who

has taught English overseas can attest, the job isn't so much "work" as something you do to support binge drinking and weekend trips to surrounding countries.

But touring in a rock and roll band? Sticking together to play music might sound idealistic, but it's harder work than many might assume. It means spending long stretches of time away from those close to you. It means leaving the comforts of home not because you want to, but because contractual and financial obligations require you to. It's clear that The Hip enjoy touring, as they've continued to do it for over twenty years. But on that night in Utrecht, it was as if the band didn't want to be anywhere but back home.

I can never fault the band for having an off day. For the thirteen years I'd been religiously following them prior to that evening in Utrecht, I had faith that not only could they provide me with direction in the world, but could save the world entirely. Their music had always inspired me cerebrally; it was music not just with brains but with balls to match. I went to Europe to learn about life; it took that trip to learn something I had overlooked about the band. The five members of The Tragically Hip were only human. They were five grown men, cathartically dealing with emotions on a stage. And as every father, brother, janitor or angry drunk in the corner can attest, dealing with emotions isn't something many men can do easily, even in the privacy of their own home. Utrecht, one of the worst Hip gigs I'd ever attended, showed the band's heart.

Leaving Canada for Europe had been an easy choice. Deciding to spend a week following The Hip across Western Europe had been even easier. Yet the band's decision to stick together, while fairly idealistic in nature, cannot be the easiest part of their job.

I thought that by living and travelling like a touring band, I could truly understand the lifestyle. My anger at the band's awful final performance still gave way to a new level of respect for The Hip. But as my flight from Warsaw took off for Toronto, I thought about the country both myself and the band were returning to, and how that same country was now, paradoxically enough, oceans apart.

"When you talk about The Hip you have to talk about their fans, too. They are the most loyal fans there are. And the most passionate. And they've carried the band through an incredibly long and also growing career. The one thing I notice when I see them play these days is that there's a whole new generation of fans out there. It's been passed down from parents to children and so on. And the new fans are as passionate and dedicated in that way. And that's the mark of a great band, one that manages to reach across those generational lines and find a way to speak to young people. Sometimes you're lucky enough to be standing on the stage, watching them play and looking out at these teenage faces, shouting and singing back the lyrics to songs that are well beyond their lifetime at this point."

— *Sam Roberts,* What It's Like to Tour With The Tragically Hip, *The Toronto Star, Friday, July 22, 2016*

CHAPTER 10

Remember, it's Only Music

Admittedly, there are more important things in my life now than The Tragically Hip. But these things didn't exist during the height of my obsession with the band. And any excitement I feel now still doesn't hold a candle to the outright bliss I used to experience when seeing The Hip live.

I may not listen to the band as religiously as I once did, but the person I am today exists because of their music. Perhaps that's what's really important: not the music itself, but the legacy it creates. After all, music becomes more disposable by the day, but what stays permanent is the personal mythology that each fan creates around a band.

Somewhere, someone is getting drunk for the first time with music in the background from a band no one has even heard of. (I bet it's happening in Leduc, Alberta. Just a hunch.) And one day, that band might be the biggest thing in the world.

And someone, right now, is driving alone in their parent's car for the first time. The stereo is cranked well beyond a reasonable volume and the driver (who really, really loves this song) is probably paying considerably less attention to the road than he or she should. Personal safety cast aside in the face of a new love.

Everyone remembers exactly where they were when these rites of passage occurred. But for some, the background music is so closely entwined with the event that the music becomes an immoveable part of the memory.

◆◆◆

Released in May 1997, *Live Between Us* dominated my boombox during those impressionable years of puberty and was still in heavy rotation when I was sixteen. And the record was around when my on-again, off-again girlfriend, who lived around the corner from me (geography probably had the biggest impact on our relationship), began to break down in the face of my constant and predictable efforts to lose our virginity together.

It was a confusing afternoon. Her mother and sister weren't home and neither of us had any homework, so all of the necessary prerequisites were met. We had contemplated the matter for long enough. We both held on to the idea that what was about to happen ought to be perfect, so we thought we should have some music. Her musical interests revolved mostly around Backstreet Boys and that Alanis Morissette record; nothing that both of us could agree on.

I dug into my backpack and put *Live Between Us* in her tiny CD player. Albums that memorable inspire you both mentally and physically. She refused at first, but eventually relented as the album opened with the smooth, intoxicating build of "Grace, too." It was cheap seduction with the aid of a blues-influenced rock and roll band. But boys, when faced with their first sexual experience, cannot be held accountable for their lack of consideration.

Through the first six songs we fumbled and wondered aloud about whether it should happen. It finally did as the seventh track, "The Luxury," kicked in. I had always hated that song. It had no groove; I couldn't mimic celebrity alone in my room along with it. But the opening, rumbling bass line accompanied my foray into the great unknown. And it was all over by the time the first chorus kicked in. My very first sexual failure. I loved *Live Between Us* even more, but still loathed that stupid song just as much.

We both sat in awkward silence, wondering if what had transpired was everything it could have been. Three minutes later, "The Luxury" finished and "Courage" began. To this day, the chorus, now steeped in irony, reminds me of that moment:

> "Courage/My word/It couldn't come at a worse time"

◆◆◆

Skipping school for the first time is another hallowed rite of passage. Some people skip rather often. Me, I was unnecessarily preoccupied with my academic reputation. It wasn't until the eleventh grade that I decided to skip class. I'd been psyching myself up for weeks for this inaugural act of rebellion.

After all, why should I have to wait until after school to rush to the HMV in the Oshawa Centre mall to pick up *Music at Work*? Why couldn't I just leave during Mr. Beharrell's second period English class?

I could barely sit still on the bus. I hadn't told anyone I was skipping; I felt daring and independent all at once. And how promising *Music at Work* was; this was to be the first new Hip release I'd buy since I had first seen them live. Three of the tracks they debuted the night of my first concert would end up on the album. I already felt a special kinship with the record and the bus had barely chugged away from my high school's parking lot.

I was turning over a new leaf. Skipping class was a big deal; now I could claim I'd done it, instead of shying away when the topic was brought up. And I was going to own a Hip record that, when memorized, would become the soundtrack to my life. I had found inspiration to break the mold thanks to the band.

How cool I felt wandering nonchalantly back into the cafeteria near the end of lunch. (What good is a trip to the mall without a stop at the food court?) Casually, I boasted that I'd skipped to pick up the new Hip record.

"You're crazy Josh," I was mocked. "What does the mall close at three o'clock or something?"

They couldn't touch me. I rode that high for the rest of the week.

And here's the kicker: *Music at Work* had been leaked three months earlier. I'd been spinning burned copies the entire time. When I actually had the disc in my hands, albeit when I should have been mulling over some of The Bard's finer work in Mr. Beharrell's class, I already knew all the words.

Though The Hip inspired me to do these things, what really matters is that they happened. That The Hip were there with me didn't make them memorable, just *more* memorable. I hope I would remember losing my virginity and skipping school for the first time if Iron Maiden (or even complete silence) was in the background. It's just reassuring to know that this band of five dudes mattered that much to me to be there, too.

◆◆◆

There are certain elements of your childhood that stay with you forever. I still crave Kraft Dinner and hotdogs, though usually when I'm hungover. And I've now graduated to Chorizo sausage.

Like so many other dudes from the Southern Ontario suburbs, I was raised on a steady diet of the Toronto Maple Leafs. Even as a youngster, I believed I needed to become personally involved with the Leafs in order to ensure their success. The Leafs were a source of happiness, sorrow and anticipation for me. Eventually, The Hip became the source of those same emotions.

For whatever reason, I lost touch with my favourite hockey team along the way. Perhaps I only had enough room for one obsession. It wasn't until I moved to Vancouver in the fall of 2008 that I rediscovered my team and how gratifying it was to follow their every move. I enjoyed being the underdog, as the Leafs were consistently put to shame by the Vancouver Canucks. The Leafs, like The Hip, became part of my identity in the city of Vancouver.

The Hip have long been associated with hockey. It's almost a guarantee that you'll hear a Hip track during a stoppage in play at nearly every NHL game in Canada. The band have written three tracks rich with hockey references: "Fifty Mission Cap," "Fireworks," (which was originally titled "Bobby Orr") and "The Lonely End of the Rink." *Road Apples*, their second album was named after a slang term for frozen horse shit used as hockey pucks in small-town Canada. If that isn't enough, Gord Downie is the godson of Hall of Famer Harry Sinden, who coached Team Canada to victory over the Soviets in the 1972 Summit Series. Downie wore a homemade Boston Bruins sweater in the music video for "Courage," an homage to his favourite team. I was reluctant to associate The Hip with hockey, believing it a simplistic tag that reinforced the idea that The Hip were a band only for Canadians. Eventually though, I came to accept that hockey was a natural fit for the band's workingman aesthetic.

2010 was a good year to be a hockey fan in Canada. After Sidney Crosby cemented his place in Canadian history with his overtime goal to capture the Olympic Gold Medal over the Americans, I became immersed in all things hockey yet again. I entered the 2010-2011 season with a sense of heightened expectation. I was a full-fledged fan again, eager to shoulder the highs and lows that come with a season supporting my childhood heroes.

A few weeks before the beginning of the hockey season, I was granted the opportunity to interview Downie for a monthly music magazine. I had pushed hard for it, knowing it would be an opportunity to speak to him outside the confines of being an obsessed fan.

Downie was an intimidating interview subject. He gave intense, thoughtful answers to every question I asked. As I had expected, our interview ran long and I had to cut some of my planned questions, including which team Gord believed would come out of the Northeast division. In hindsight, I'm glad I didn't get a chance to ask, since he was later asked a similar question by respected radio DJ Dave Bookman. When I read the transcript of the interview, his answer haunted me for weeks:

"Well, you know Bookie, I'm trying to kick hockey. I'm on the patch."

Downie outlined some of the problems with the modern game and showed little of the passion that he seemed to have had for it in the past. It didn't make sense to me. One of the driving creative forces behind The Hip was distancing himself from an element of the band's aesthetic that I had long resisted, but now embraced.

I wallowed in self-pity over Gord's revelation, only to realize that it was The Hip's music that helped me become the man I am today (nothing too noble, but still better than the zit-speckled kid who worshipped Doug Gilmour's every forecheck), and it was the music that should speak louder than Gord and my personal differences of opinion. Hockey was an inescapable part of the band's repertoire, inasmuch as it is a part of the country that both the band and I call home.

Yet, it's only *part* of the band and the country. While "Fifty Mission Cap" was the song that hooked me onto

The Hip, the tragedy it speaks of is almost sixty years old. Like any good friendship, my relationship with The Hip has evolved. And what keeps a fan like me coming back is what brought me to them in the first place: the records and the concerts they give to fans, year after year. The Leafs could have been in the dumps in that stretch between '92 and '94, when I first got into the band, and it probably wouldn't have mattered.

Shortly after our interview, Downie played a gig with The Country of Miracles at the Vogue Theatre in Vancouver. Jess and I went, ending a Hip-related drought that had lasted well over a year. Gord and The Country of Miracles displayed Downie's range as an artist with country-rockers, heartfelt ballads, and whimsical bluesy jams. His passion for the songs he wrote was obvious and by the end of the night, there wasn't a fan who wasn't bouncing along to every note with a grin on their face. Though the beginning of the hockey season was just days away, Gord made no mention of it. Instead, he spoke about the struggle between "the Canada you 'know' and the Canada you 'feel.'"

The Canada I knew was in the front row, standing where I always had. And though I didn't feel the same obsession for The Hip that I once had, it was reaffirming to see Downie working hard to entertain the fans who had stuck by him.

I thought again of our interview, conducted when I was back in Oshawa for a wedding. I made the phone call from the same bedroom I had returned to after my first gig, the same room where I danced on my bed, memorizing the band's repertoire. I didn't want to out myself as a fan, but it was too tempting; I couldn't pass up the chance to ask Gord what he "got" from the fans every night. I had spent the better part of my life as a Hip fan, working hard to see them, to meet them, even to get the interview. Did Downie and the rest of the band see that work? If he didn't recognize my dedication, then I might have questioned the last fifteen years of my life. I waited expectantly for his answer.

"Something brand new," he said. "Something that's disappearing as it's happening. Something really transient. And yet cool. It's hard to describe, yet entirely vivid. It's the coming together of people for any number of reasons to have an individual, transient, and hopefully transcendent experience by yourself, in a crowd. These are things that people still search out, especially in the summertime after being cooped up in Oshawa all winter. You spend all winter dreaming it up and then you've got to get out there and express yourself. And you can express yourself simply by enjoying a moment."

Watching the gig that night, it didn't matter what I knew about Gord's feelings towards hockey. What mattered was that night and the thousands of moments we had shared, the language of his tunes that we both understood and finally, the Canada—and the entire world—that The Hip had created that we still called home.

◆◆◆

Sometimes, in moments of clarity, you can see your future. It's not of the revolutionary, Doc Brown kind, but those strange moments where your knowledge of who you are and your ideas about who you want to be collide. And there, usually while doing something out of habit, you catch a glimpse of a person that may resemble you slightly (and let's be honest: it's never all that flattering), and you realize you'll probably still be doing the things you enjoy now, twenty, twenty-five or maybe fifty years down the road.

At a midnight showing of *Charlie Is My Darling*, a rare Rolling Stones documentary hosted by one-time Stones manager Andrew Loog Oldham, I came face-to-face with my future. The room was full of older, out-of-shape classic rock fiends who were way too excited that the theatre was serving cans of cheap lager. And their wives were excited about being able to spend time with their husbands, while still getting in a little shut-eye.

There I sat, drinking beer in a movie theatre, quoting John Travolta in *Pulp Fiction* and nudging my girlfriend to keep her awake. I was among my people. It all made sense.

The low-quality film ended and there was a Q&A session with Oldham, the man who told The Rolling Stones, the greatest rock and roll band to ever set foot on a stage, to stop playing covers and write originals. The man was, in some way, responsible for "Jumpin' Jack Flash."

I had been thinking all day about The Stones, and ironically enough, their age. I wanted to ask Oldham about the relevance of The Stones now, and whether their status as aging, sometimes-laughable rock stars helps or hampers their legacy. I hoped his answer would give me some context about The Hip's ascension into the "aging" category of rock and rollers.

But as soon as the session began, any semblance of reason was lost. It began when one man directed his wife towards the stage to beg Oldham for autographs while he asked three questions in a row about inane technical specifications of records released over forty years previous. The rock nerds talked over and interrupted each other, and asked as many questions in a row as they could before another nerd cut them off. And the questions they asked weren't about the enduring power of the Stones' music, but ridiculous things like: "What is your relationship with Mick like?" (Oldham finished his professional relationship with the Stones in 1967.)

Would "Ruby Tuesday" sound any better if Oldham hadn't answered, "Oh, we still get on just fine"? These grown men had waited up all night for the chance to ask this man a question, all because he was affiliated for a few years with a rock and roll band.

I don't think I'm any *better* or *worse* than these fans, but as I walked home with my near comatose-from-boredom girlfriend, I realized that, unless I did something about it, this could be my future.

If you're into music, you've seen this kind of person before: someone who is so obsessed with a particular work or artist that he or she seems to forget how to actually *enjoy* the art. The type of people who own every first pressing, have paid thousands for rare imports, and know the *real* meaning behind nearly every track. But ask how a song makes them *feel* and you'll get a blank stare. For these people, getting into music is only done out of a desire to collect, not for enjoyment of the music itself. It's a road I hope I never turn down.

The feelings of anticipation I've had while waiting for The Hip to take the stage, the realization that I might very well have been in love while the band played a slow number and the utter heartache I felt when I missed a chance to shake a band member's hand were all part of the experience of loving a band enough to let them change the way I lived. But the feeling I get when I spin *Day for Night* for the thousandth time? That one is easy: complete bliss.

Sure, if Daniel Lanois, producer of *Day for Night*, hosted a midnight screening of rare footage of the band recording in 1993-1994, I'd be in the front row. But I don't care whether Gord Downie and Daniel still chat. Technical details and inside stories are all well and good and may shed a little light on a certain song, but they do not make me love the band any more than I already do. Loving a band isn't something you learn easily, however it's crucial that you always remember how to do it.

◆◆◆

When I'm asked about my greatest moment as a Hip fan (which, to be fair, rarely happens and only when I least expect it), I find it tough to regale people with stories of trudging through the coldest day of a Polish winter to find news of an impending European summer tour, or doing raunchy things with a girl I'd never see again on the lawns at Molson Amphitheatre, though these stories exemplify the kind of pain and redemption that makes you a hit at parties.

Instead, I usually think about the first job I ever had, delivering twenty-five copies of the *Oshawa Times* three days a week. My first paycheque was enough for bus fare to the Oshawa Centre, a copy of *Trouble at the Henhouse*, a meal in the food court, and bus fare back home. Not being obsessed yet, I didn't need *Trouble at the Henhouse* to round out my psyche. I was just twelve years old and hearing "Ahead by a Century" brought a smile to my face, without complication.

With age comes an excuse for everything: not having enough disposable income, always having something to do around the house or any number of other excuses to not do things like attend gigs or essentially, enjoy yourself without consequence.

The Hip was always about the refutation of my excuses. There was always an exam I should have been studying for, a shortage of cash, or the notion that getting into a car with complete strangers for the sake of a rock and roll gig was socially unacceptable behaviour. But those gigs were the source of a high that may have turned a bored suburban kid off hard drugs (or worse, complacency) for his entire life.

In the beginning, there was simply so much to discover and understand. I think it's fitting that I really got into the band during puberty. After all, not only was I coming of age, The Hip, who had been playing music for as long as I'd been alive, were also finding their unique voice as well.

The Hip brought me so much joy that it became hard to spend time with other bands. Sure, I grew up on a steady diet of my father's classic rock (The Who, Rush) and '90s radio rock (Pearl Jam, R.E.M, Live) but there was so much depth and mystery to The Hip that it became difficult for me to spread my love around.

Once The Hip started bringing opening bands on tour that really seduced me, I realized that there was more to music than The Hip. It took a long time to come to this realization. Yet because of my love for The Hip, when I actually did start to invest my time in other bands, a strange thing happened. My love for The Hip didn't really disappear; that love just grew onto the world of rock and roll as a whole.

Close to twenty years since I first started listening to The Hip, they're in a different league altogether. It's not easy to get out of the bottom of the music journalism food chain but without The Hip I wouldn't even be hungry. And it's not as if every new record I spin or every concert I attend is held against them. That's unfair to the time I invested getting to know The Hip, the world of music, and myself. The Hip have been the cagey, all-knowing parents who taught me everything I know at home, but were never able to leave the house to see me put that knowledge to work.

"We played a little more with Sam Roberts before we played with The Hip. And Sam is such a leader. And he always treats everybody really kindly and makes time for everybody. And he knows that when he goes out, people are going to want his time. And he makes a point of being generous and thoughtful. I was having a conversation about that with Jack Ross, our agent. And Jack says, 'Oh, Sam learned all of that from The Hip.' When Sam was in our position, he toured with The Hip countless times. And The Hip were totally of that school. You have to be aware that your interactions mean something with the people you cross. Obviously the Arkells aren't on that level but it's something I take with me: if somebody goes out of their way to introduce themselves to the band and say something nice, they are putting themselves out there. I should honour that."

— *Max Kerman, Arkells*

CHAPTER 11

The Beginning of the End

I spent much of 2007-2008 abroad, far removed from The Hip. Throughout that year, I went from simply missing that part of my life to mourning its loss.

It was exciting, then, to return to Canada alone. After a few days spent catching up with family, I left Oshawa and headed for Ottawa to stay with good friends and catch the band at the week-long outdoor Ottawa Bluesfest.

Heading east along the 401, I thought about the year since I'd last seen the band live. I wondered how much both the band and my friends had changed. Al, who had accompanied me to London in '04, had moved in with a girl and was on the road to marriage. It was with a heavy heart and a lead foot that I pined for those long-ago carefree days of our friendship in Guelph.

Four of us, including Al and his girlfriend, Alison, wandered to the festival grounds a few hours before The Hip's set. It took just half a set of their classics, infused with the light-hearted vibe of summer that surrounded us, for me to remember just how amiable their concerts could be. My reverse culture-shock slowly began to fade away, at least enough to relax and enjoy the moment. I looked around for validation, but instead, found hesitation in Al and Alison's demeanour, as we drank cups of foamy, over-priced festival beer. They kept eyeing their watches, looking for the right moment to say what they probably didn't want to:

"Well, we have to get up early tomorrow morning. Maybe we should go."

I anxiously smoked a cigarette, as the band, far from being finished, continued to work their magic onstage, ploughing through a barrage of their greatest hits.

If they had decided to play rarities all night, I might have understood their desire to jump ship. But the band was playing a set designed for casual onlookers. And away walked my old friend, who had taken a chance on our friendship and let it blossom over a two-hour trip to a Hip show four years earlier. While the band hadn't created our relationship, it acted as the spark, and as such, all future Hip concerts we attended together would have a heightened importance. Watching him leave was like saying goodbye to the wide-eyed second-year students we'd been only a few years before. Worse yet, it felt like we'd let the spirit of those kids down.

The band returned for an encore with a cover of David Bowie's "Queen Bitch," which was probably a highlight for many in attendance. I stood unmoved though: "Queen Bitch" had been one of the final songs at my last Hip gig. I'd now heard it three times live. Given that the band had only played the track a handful of times in a live setting, I should have been a very happy camper.

Maybe I would have been more enthusiastic if Al had still been there, but he'd moved on. Bands have a way of forming direct relationships with the listener; there's a love that only you can experience. But when bands act as the glue of shared memory in relationships, that relationship becomes quite tenuous. And it wasn't like Al was the only guy who'd ever let anyone down—I'd done my fair share too. I once took in a Pearl Jam gig with Ol' Smokey and got too drunk to remember Ben Harper coming onstage. But Smokey remembers. Now we have two different memories, not the same one, and our friendship suffers because of it. We've lost a moment. We've lost something in common. For a concert fan, it's a great pain.

Al and I will share many stories of our London '04 gig before we'd even think of speaking of Ottawa '08. We'd had the London gig in common. That Ottawa Hip gig was the first I'd seen in a year, but it was the first time I missed the company more than the band I thought I'd travelled to see.

◆◆◆

After The Hip's fruitless *We Are The Same* (though the thoughtful trance of "The Depression Suite" did get me through many a long morning) and my relocation to Vancouver in 2008, I fell out of touch with The Hip. Living near the band's home base had always served me well, but now, I was a citizen of a strange place where my lack of exposure to the band directly severed my connection. I lived in a city where the band only toured sporadically: fewer gigs, lowered obsession. Now out of sight, The Hip soon became out of mind. I began to look at bands critically, instead of with unfailing adoration. And as such, the world of music became more of a new frontier to discover and less of a commodity that I defined myself by.

The dichotomy I was experiencing came to a head in June of 2009. The band was coming to Vancouver for three nights at the atmospheric Orpheum Theatre. It was The Hip who inspired me to "look for a place to happen," and in Vancouver, I felt as if I'd finally found it. The band would soon also play Abbotsford, a town not one hour's drive from where I lived. Years before, I wouldn't have thought twice about making the drive to the gig alone. But now, what mattered more than being with those who appreciated me simply as a voice in the crowd was being in the company of those whose influence was personal. The Hip's music hadn't lost any of its quality, though it had lost some of its influence.

After the second Vancouver gig, I sat in a bar, waiting for Jess to meet me, jotting down what I remembered of the setlist on a napkin, just as I'd done after my first Hip gig. As I sipped my beer, I found it hard to recapture that same ecstatic post-gig feeling.

Jess walked into the bar. I'd been thinking of her throughout the gig. It was a little distracting at first, until I realized that I was checking my watch every few songs, wondering when I could leave to see her. I tucked the napkin into my pocket.

It may sound as though I was trading one love for another. But when I put the napkin away, I realized that The Hip were just for me now, and always would be. And no matter how long you live and how many loves you have and share, you never forget your first.

◆◆◆

Less than a year after returning to Canada, I'd struck gold. Vancouver's largest daily newspaper, The Vancouver Sun, hired me to do freelance work. Covering gigantic concerts and filing stories on tight deadlines was thrilling. I thought I was on my way to Lester Bangs-style stardom, and would soon be hobnobbing with the most elusive of bands.

How quickly I'd forgotten that I'd only written for my university newspaper for a year, and for eight months after that, a monthly magazine on the other side of the world. It didn't take long before calls from the Sun became less and less frequent. And this lack of work seemed to coincide with The Hip's return to Vancouver for the Orpheum gigs.

I believed that with my extensive knowledge of the band, I'd be able to write the perfect review of their first night in town. My editor, however, wanted nothing to do with my pitch. I was turned down for the gig, forced to sit home and stew, having only grabbed tickets to the last two of the three shows, while my replacement covered the gig.

The next morning, I read the article in disgust. Not only had the writer failed to spell Gord Downie's name correctly, he had failed to realize that The Hip were still touring, and how important a part of their legacy that was. I was furious. I reread the piece on my way home after work, rewriting it in my mind.

It soon became clear that I couldn't have written the review in only five hundred words. For me to adequately express my admiration of the band's back catalogue while reporting on the night's events would have been impossible. When it came to The Hip, I couldn't report accurately. My obsession would shine through. I realized that my anger stemmed from my inability to bring this love into my burgeoning writing career. The Hip had turned me onto music, but I couldn't integrate that original spark into my work as a music journalist. I was still angry as the lights went down for the next night's gig.

I stood at attention as always, eager to hear the band in a new venue. But with my lingering emotional attachment, taking notes and subsequently leaving my seat to file those notes would have been impossible.

Most of the crowd remained seated for "The Depression Suite," the opener. People sitting behind me hurled insults, imploring me to sit down. But I couldn't. I couldn't enjoy this gig and not sing out loud either. I was twenty-five but still sixteen at heart. I was trying to become a music journalist, but these gigs made one thing abundantly clear: When it comes to this band, I'm not the professional type. I'm not the backstage schmoozer. I don't know anyone in the band or have any connections.

I'm the guy who waits behind the venue in the pouring rain just to shake a member of the band's hand and say thanks for all the work they've done. I'm the one who gets drunk at weddings and implores DJs to play the band's hits. I'm a fan.

And perhaps I was a certain *kind* of fan. Because I believed, with all my heart, that I would be the best person to tell The Hip's story. That my passion, coupled with the band's friendly, welcoming demeanour, would enable me to cross boundaries. I imagined a life where I followed the band on the road and learned how they lived and brought their show to the fans. I could be the one to introduce them to a younger generation, to keep their music alive in the wake of flashes-in-the pan and one-hit wonders.

It took me over twenty years of being a fan and a decade of attending gigs to realize that people like me are already part of the band in a strange but irreplaceable way. Fans perform for the band as much as the other way around. But what those Vancouver gigs made me realize is that usually, the connection ends there. When bands and fans do meet, it's special, but also rare.

Those two Vancouver gigs were my last foreseeable Hip gigs. Lately, I prefer to spend my time in grungy bars with young bands looking for their big break. But sometimes, when I'm at a show in some dank bar, engrossed in the music, I know The Hip aren't so far away. The venues may have changed, but I wouldn't be hanging out there, or be who I am today without the band, who got their start in those same kinds of bars, many years ago. And although I always assumed that a fan was the best person to tell a band's story, I was wrong. The only story I can tell is my own.

Epilogue

In January 2013 I returned to Toronto after two years in Southeast Asia and Australia, foolishly thinking that the paltry music writing I had done years before would be able to translate into the professional life I'd dreamt about. But this was not the case. I'd read writers younger than me writing for publications that I dreamt of working at, but who wouldn't take my calls no matter how many times I dialled. If The Tragically Hip have taught me anything it's that matters of the heart, especially those that involve a homecoming, rarely work out as planned.

My professional life intersected with my private life when The Hip played Oshawa less than two weeks after I returned from Australia. I felt nervous pangs at not being privy to at least one Hip show as I furiously typed off emails to everyone I knew within The Hip's camp to get on the guest list.

Even over three years removed from my last Hip show, I still believed I was something of a failure if I wasn't taking part in the circus that is still a Hip tour during a long Canadian winter.

Yet, as I entered the General Motors Centre with the other amateur photographers, I wasn't entirely sure why I was in attendance. Was I taking in my umpteenth Hip show because it kept my sanity in check and provided me with closure, or was this show bettering me in some way?

I waited for The Hip to take the stage, alone and afraid. I would return that evening to the house I grew up in. On Monday morning I'd go to a job I hated and return that same Monday evening to my parents' home. I was quickly approaching 30 and my wide-eyed optimism had been traded for the stark reality that, in starting up from scratch again, I couldn't expect anything to be handed to me.

In the past, the moments before a show were often the most engaging because as a fan I maintained the ability to totally give in to anticipation. But now, I was scared shitless, pining anxiously for a cigarette.

Though The Hip drew a sizeable crowd that night in Oshawa, the truth was, there were many bands that would've drawn a more sizeable and enthusiastic crowd; bands that the very writers I envied were shedding light on. The Hip's day in the sun had passed, and I feared that mine had too.

Sure, it was once completely acceptable to give in to a song, a band or even a movement for reasons unclear and simply enjoy the ride, wherever it would take you. Perhaps you could allow this momentum to develop into a passion you maintained with ardency. But there comes a time when that obsession must be examined from a critical angle. What effect did this obsession have permanently, if at all? And if it didn't have an effect, was being a fan simply a phase you were destined to grow out of?

The band sauntered onstage as they always do. I was standing in the photo pit, closer than anyone else in the arena. But the band wouldn't smile at me. Something had changed. There were more questions than answers.

Knowing then that my belief in The Tragically Hip had changed, was I to forget about my aspirations and assume I'd gone the way of the dinosaurs? And then likewise give up on the band I grew up with, allowing them to go the way of casino-bound nostalgia-driven acts? That, I worried, would degrade the music that inspired me to begin writing, travelling and living the life I wanted in the first place.

Not long after that Oshawa gig, I visited the Horseshoe Tavern in Toronto with my best friend. We watched in amazement at a country singer, singing songs we once scoffed at with a sense of conviction that I long thought was unattainable.

"What happened?" I asked my friend afterwards. "I used to turn my head at country music, but I couldn't stop watching those guys."

"I know what you mean," he said. "These older bands are the only ones we can learn anything from anymore. Newer, younger acts don't really have anything to teach us because we've already been there. Now I know why our dads still listen to the same music they did when they were our age, those bands will always seem a little older and a little wiser."

Good music is permanent. And if there's one universal trend of Canadian music, it's that it's encouraging. While the trails of America have been paved a thousand times over, there are still many within Canada that have not. It may be a rite of passage for Canadians to drive across the country, but the rite of passage should not be just to go across, but to go up and down, to get lost and to find everything in between. I don't know much about places like Cold Lake, Red Deer, St. John's, and Penticton. I'd like to say I do. But what I do know about them is that The Hip have played there. And when I learn that they have, or they will, the first thing I do is read about these cities. I don't worry about how The Hip will go over, because I know the impression they make does not end when the band walks offstage.

The Hip's music may be delivered in hockey arenas and make-shift stages over fields littered with cigarette butts and plastic beer cups. But their voice truly finds its legs at the campfires where their songs are sung late into the night, where old friends find a common bond sharing honesty in coarse, throaty tones. I don't fear meeting someone new anymore because I know, somewhere deep in the recesses of their (and mine, sure) drunken state of mind, we can probably agree that "Wheat Kings" is a story worth conversing about. Because "Three Pistols" got us more interested in Canadian mythology than any history class ever has. Because we all fell in love, in some way or another, with "Ahead by a Century" lingering in the background. Because we've all gotten stoned and heard *Day for Night*. The Tragically Hip, their music having evolved into a common language spoken amongst kindred spirits far and wide, are not a band that only people that were born within a few years of me will understand. Fans can learn about each other because of what we've learned from the band.

Sure, The Tragically Hip close to thirty years after their inception may not be the influential act they once were. But perception being nine-tenths of reality, The Hip's importance has grown because it continues to inspire a smaller group of ardent fans more than it would if it were spread out thinner amongst the masses.

Those ardent fans watched in adoration as the band built up steam back in Oshawa. The Hip as a band were older than many of the fans in attendance but they continued to surprise people.

The world The Hip exposed me to has taught me many things, though if the band themselves have taught me anything, it's not to quit. They refuse to become a novelty casino act and as a fan, being able to continue learning from your obsession is the best reason to believe in said obsession.

I cannot worry at great length about The Tragically Hip because they are not finished. And as Gord Downie promised me at my first Hip show, they are never going away. Many bands younger than The Hip throw in the towel without near the output or daring that The Hip have shown. As the band closed their Oshawa show with a rousing "The Lookahead" and a thundering "Blow at High Dough," I felt rejuvenated knowing there are artists like The Hip who refuse to go quietly into the night, continue to take risks, perform relentlessly regardless of age or mass popularity, and inspire generations of fans.

Some nights live music is made to be fun, most nights it's capable of so much more. Let's reserve the past for those who have left us, and embrace those that can push on through the uncertain future with pride and promise. And grace, too.

Post Script

The morning of May 24th was not a pleasant one for Tragically Hip fans. So many of us awoke to a text from a friend, a social media update, or a hastily delivered news broadcast and came to a startling realization: The Tragically Hip would not be with us forever. The band announced that lead singer Gord Downie had been diagnosed with terminal brain cancer, putting their long term future in doubt.

Believing that this band would become the first ever immortal rock 'n' roll act was foolish. But up until that morning, through over thirty years of their career and thousands of shows across the world, The Tragically Hip had made an incredible and incredibly rare leap: in the eyes and hearts of their fans, they were not a band of unattainable musicians. They were people whom you interacted with on your own level, perhaps every day.

And fans of The Tragically Hip, whether or not they had ever met Gord Downie, felt like they were losing a friend.

Quickly, Downie and the band were eulogized in the media and reports of their upcoming tour being their "final" one were incorrectly published. The Tragically Hip's management, even after hosting a news conference with

Downie's neuro-oncologist Dr. James Perry, never stated clearly that their 2016 summer tour to promote Man Machine Poem would be their last. As such, it was difficult for many fans to put a finger on the emotions swelling that day. I spoke with many media outlets but the one agreement I came to was with my friend and Toronto Star music critic Ben Rayner: there was no real precedent for what was happening.

To be clear: fans, by and large, wanted to grieve. Although I spent nearly every interview I did that day reminding anyone who would listen that this was not, explicitly, the band's last tour, many people I spoke to had skipped straight to the fourth stage of grief: tear-in-yer-beer depression.

In a year in which the music world had already lost Prince and David Bowie, news of Gord Downie's terminal cancer struck Canadians in particular with a strangely selfish sense of grief. "We really don't ask for much," said the Canadian. "Why are you taking one of the few things I can call my own away from me?"

And inevitably, from unnecessary eulogy came the mythology-building. Calls for Downie to receive the Order of Canada came out. Musicians that had been impacted by Downie and The Tragically Hip spoke glowingly of their experiences with him and the band. Some recorded tributes. City councillors proposed using public funds to throw large-scale concerts not included on the Canadian tour. Seemingly everywhere, everyone wanted a piece of Downie and The Hip.

Losing something close to you is a horrifically painful experience. But slowly losing something that you were once close to is a strange process. Every Tragically Hip fan has his or her own connection to the band, even if that connection was born years ago and is now mostly a memory. How do music fans grieve the loss of a memory?

For most of their career, The Tragically Hip were defined less by their music and more by their fans the loud, puffed-chest fans who proudly waved their red and white flags and showed up en masse across the country and the planet. But like Insane Clown Posse's Juggalos and Jugalettes and the Grateful Dead's Deadheads, fans of The Tragically Hip could also be dedicated, passionate, and warm to their kind, even though they were often viewed as outcasts.

As such, despite their popularity throughout Canada, being a fan of The Tragically Hip was always an exercise in exclusivity. Because The Hip were never accepted by popular American culture, fans of the band got to live the greatest secret in the music business at every show. It was dependable, and it was heartfelt. "Canada's house band" they were called. A Tragically Hip show was less of a place to be entertained and more of a venue to come together with friends, not unlike your favourite local watering hole.

Eventually, as the band's career progressed into the 2000s and they moved away from chunky, barn-burning rock tracks and towards introspective, slow-paced tracks that took time to grow, so too did their audience change. Songs about hockey were replaced by songs that, while hidden in Downie's cryptic poetry, called for social change.

The Tragically Hip's latest record, Man Machine Poem, is rich with sonic subtleties. It doesn't bludgeon you over the head as past Hip releases have. It's very much representative of the band: refusing to be pigeonholed and always interested in what strange, beautiful places their music will go next. And as their music continued to evolve from the radio-ready rock of their early career, scores of the Canadian music industry's most admired musicians began jumping on the bandwagon.

In a series of tweets after Downie's diagnosis was revealed, Damian Abraham, the lead singer of Toronto-based punk act Fucked Up said, "In a music industry full of liars, shitheads, and monsters, Gord Downie is one of the few beacons of light. He cares and believes in a way that makes me envious. As a young person I dismissed him and his band simply because I didn't like some of their fans. Nothing has illustrated the folly of youth better for me than coming to know and appreciate him and his work."

Abraham worked with Downie on Fucked Up's 2014 album Glass Boys. Downie was featured on "The Art of Patrons," singing "It's the privilege of mass delusion" repeatedly. That Downie would sing a line so loaded with context, one that could be interpreted as a reference to deluding scores of Tragically Hip fans about the band's lifelong intentions, is not lost on me. Perhaps the Tragically Hip best known as pliers of songs meant only to swig beer to was just an illusion. Maybe the Tragically Hip of 2016, the tender, introspective bunch, are the band they've always wanted to be.

Either way, your version of The Tragically Hip is important: this is a band that was able to break down cultural barriers that they never even created.

At a Tragically Hip show, you can choose to immerse yourself in the intricacies of Downie's lyrics, bang on to Paul Langlois's eternally chunky riffs, light a dart with friends of yesteryear, sing calmly to the quiet, new material or share stories of past shows with, well anyone. You can fall in love, as I have. You can be whoever the hell you want to be.

Because now, there is a Tragically Hip for everyone.

All of this was first referenced by Downie himself in a poem titled "We Are The Next Us," which was posted on the band's website in 2005. One stanza stuck out to me:

Go to a show.
Music Lovers under a full moon in trust
It's not the band you like it's their sea of hate you don't trust
you're in the right place

The band's songs are open to your own personal interpretation and can be anything you want them to be but in the end, they are not yours and yours alone. And as fans, we should be thankful that the band created such an inclusive environment for their music to be shared.

The connection that fans of The Tragically Hip have to the band and to each other will truly define this band's legacy. Rare is the band that can command both a loyal following and attract new fans by evolving throughout their career. For fans of The Tragically Hip, the opportunity to stand up with pride and share their intimate connection with others has become less of a rite of passage and more of a badge of honour. It doesn't matter if The Tragically Hip's 2016 tour is their last: what is important is how they united an entire country through love, admiration, and memories.

Years from now, The Tragically Hip's music will not be any better or worse. But it will be the connections that this band has formed that will be cherished long after they play their final note onstage.

"We are never going away," Downie told me on the first day of 2000. I, for one, still believe him.

Acknowledgements

A lot of folks have bought me a drink, lent an eye or an ear, and generally given me the kind of support that's helped get this ship off to sea. I couldn't have done it without you: Sarah Kloke, David Trumble, Demetris Astritis, Wesley Craine, Huelah Lander, Adam Nielsen, Mackenzie Brisbois, Ashley Siddall and Al Gregory, Jen Hale for her guidance, Jenn Farrell for her original edits and constant positivity, Alan Cross, Ian Gormely and Jason Schneider for their kind words, my parents for everything, Deanna Smith, Johnny Fay, Gord Sinclair, Paul Langlois, Rob Baker, Gord Downie, everyone else in The Hip's camp. So many people shared kind words on May 24th, 2016. You know who you are and I thank you. Carla Gillis offered me a place to try and make sense of everything on that day, and the months afterwards. She is a fantastic editor and an even better friend. If this book is any good at all, it's because of Adam Kesek. Finally, as always, Jess, for standing beside me in the Horseshoe on August 20th, dancing to "Long Time Running" at the wedding, and being beside me every other step along the way.

About the Author

Joshua Kloke is a Toronto-based writer and teacher. His writing has appeared in *The Toronto Star*, *The Guardian*, *The Globe and Mail*, *The National Post*, *NOW Magazine* and *SI.com.*